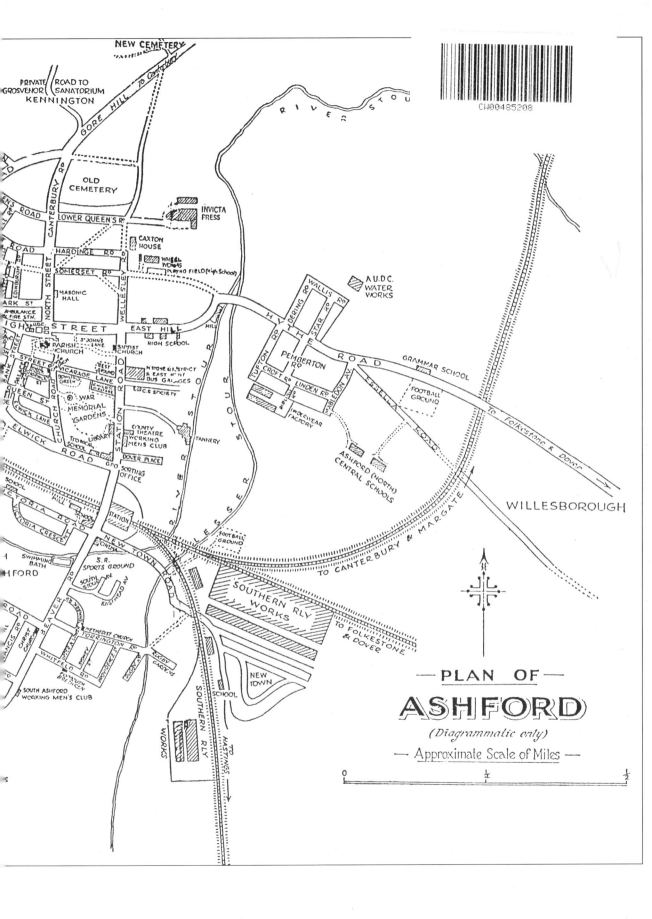

— PLAN OF —

ASHFORD

(Diagrammatic only)

— Approximate Scale of Miles —

A History of
ASHFORD

A typical view of old Ashford. The front to the Man of Kent *on the right is Victorian, but otherwise the buildings are part of the old market centre.*

A History of
ASHFORD

Arthur Ruderman

Phillimore

1994

Published by
PHILLIMORE & CO. LTD.
Shopwyke Manor Barn, Chichester

ISBN 0 85033 878 6

Printed and bound in Great Britain by
BIDDLES LTD
Guildford, Surrey

Contents

List of Illustrations

Acknowledgements

When I first became interested in the history of Ashford over twenty-five years ago, there was very little available in print. The only general history was that written by A.J. Pearman (published in three editions, the last early in this century), and that is largely a history of the church.

Wider interest was stimulated by classes under the leadership of Dr. H.C.F. Lansberry, later of the School of Continuing Education of the University of Kent at Canterbury. Others have followed him, and a class has been held in many of the years since.

As a result a number of books and pamphlets have been written, on specific subjects. This book is an attempt to give those interested a general introduction to the social and economic life of the town and its inhabitants, with sufficient background to enable those who are new to the subject to understand the importance of some of the events against the wider county and national background. In addition the intention is to make more readily available some of the documents that have been discovered in various repositories (particularly the Centre for Kentish Studies, formerly County Archives Office at Maidstone) in the hope that others will be encouraged to become interested and to carry the research still further.

The research reported in this book could not have been carried out without the help and co-operation of many people. Firstly, Dr. Fred Lansberry, whose class on Ashford I joined more than twenty-five years ago, and who has given continual support ever since.

Then there are the staffs of many record repositories and libraries. Of these, the Kent Archives Office (now the Centre for Kentish Studies) under the leadership of Dr. Felix Hull, Dr. Nigel Yates and now Kath Topping, is the most important, but many others have played their part. I express my thanks to all those who have worked in those offices over the years, not forgetting those behind the scenes who must have fetched and returned many hundredweights of records for me to use.

So many individuals and companies have allowed me to see some of their records, or have allowed me to copy and reproduce photographs and other items that I have decided not to try to list all the names here since the risk of accidentally omitting some is so great. This also avoids the problem of acknowledgement where the same photograph is available from more than one source. I hope that this course will not be seen as diminishing in any way my sincere appreciation and gratitude to everyone who has helped. I shall continue to be grateful to anyone who is able to give future help by making sources available to me.

Lastly, may I repeat that I hope that this book will enable others to continue research, and so to add to known history of the town. I accept responsibility for any errors, and shall be pleased to hear of any corrections or additions that readers may like to make.

Arthur Ruderman

March 1994

1

The Beginning

When we consider the history of this country and talk of the earliest times we must remember to keep this in perspective. We have very few documents older than 1,000 years, and very few archaeological finds are more than 1,000 years before that. Compare these periods with

- East African man circa one million years ago
- Swanscombe man circa 250,000 years ago
- Lascaux cave paintings circa 15,000 years ago.

Modern dating techniques, using radio-active decay rates, have enabled more precise definition and, in many cases, suggest earlier dates for European man than those calculated by older methods. One dating of a skull found in East Germany gives an age of about 400,000 years.

There have also been recent suggestions that there are areas in England where there has been continuous settlement for c.10,000 years. Habitation is now thought to be far more widespread than past discoveries suggest—the very fact that an area was highly suitable for cultivation means that it has been occupied continuously; thus any earlier traces may well have been destroyed by later occupiers. It must be certain that, for perhaps hundreds of generations before we have any traces of occupation, primitive man would have been experimenting with ways to find food and shelter, and many mistakes would have been made before achievements such as the bronze implements and pottery dishes that have been found. Of this very long period we know nothing, and are never likely to.

Ashford was situated on the edge of the immense forest of Anderida, or the Weald (which stretched from immediately west of Great Chart across Kent and Sussex into Hampshire), in open country, on the slope of a rise, and near to the water supply of the river Stour. It would seem, therefore, to be an attractive area for primitive man to settle, since all the basic requirements for life were available. Later, when lines of communication were developing, Ashford was well placed at the south-west end of the only gap through the North Downs for a considerable distance either east or west, and with easy access both to the sea and to the north-west. Writing many centuries later, the Kentish historian Edward Hasted described the town as 'standing most pleasant and healthy, on the knoll of a hill, of a gentle ascent on every side'.

Earliest proof of occupation is provided by the discovery of a large Bronze-Age urn at Potters Corner and an axe on the golf course in 1935. There is no evidence of any permanent Roman settlement, but they undoubtedly knew the area. A Roman road from Tenterden to Canterbury ran on the line of Beaver Road in south Ashford, crossed the river just south of where the railway runs today, continued up Station Road, Wellesley Road (now part of the ring road) and so northwards through Kennington. Another Roman road ran from Lympne to the west, and crossed the first road at the end of what is now

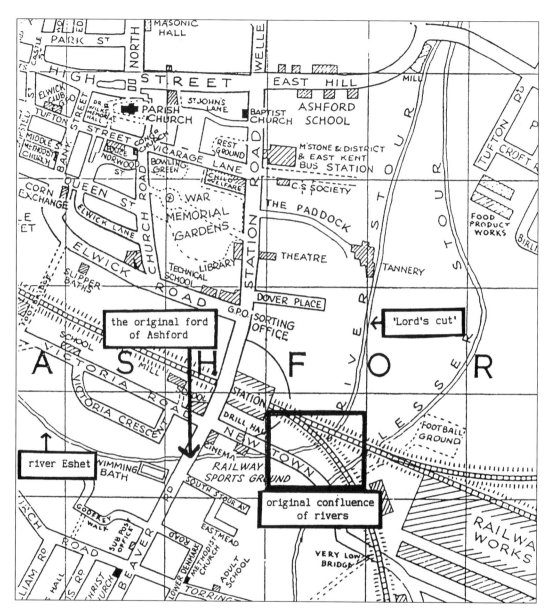

1. Map of Ashford (1935) showing the original ford and river course.

Beaver Road, at the point where the road still makes a right-angled turn to Kingsnorth. The remains of a Roman interment including a large urn and other pottery were found in 1896 when a house (now no. 33) was being built in Albert Road, and a similar burial at Potters Corner in 1929 when the main road was being widened. Other small finds have been made elsewhere in the area.

Nothing is known of the likely date for the Saxon occupation of the area, and the beginnings of the permanent settlement. There can be no doubt of the existence of a Saxon settlement at Ashford, since the name derives from them. In his book *Continuity and*

Colonization Professor Alan Everitt suggests the possibility of a settlement on the river at Ashford in the early Jutish period (about the beginning of the sixth century), but the earliest written reference (and there is even doubt as to whether this in fact does refer to Ashford) is a will of Wulfgyth dated 1053 (given by Pearman wrongly as 953), where she gives land at Essetesford to her daughter Elgyth.

Hasted says that the inhabitants of Great Chart have a tradition that Ashford rose from the ruins after that place had been burnt down by the Danes. To me this seems unlikely, since it is difficult to see how the Danes came to be in Great Chart. That they landed at Appledore in 893 is documented in the Anglo Saxon Chronicle, and after that date they undoubtedly made many raids on the coast of Kent. But some miles of thick forest separated Appledore from the Ashford area, and sea raiders such as the Danes were reluctant to penetrate so far inland, except in very open countryside. A raid on the area around Ashford is much more likely to have come from the north-east, along the valley of the Stour.

Great Chart was an estate known in documents from 762, but its population would have been very small. If the reference in Wulfgyth's will is correct it would seem likely that the first permanent settlement in Ashford was during the 10th century. The name is given in old documents as 'Essetesford' or 'Eshetisford'. Wallenberg suggests that this is derived from the Old English 'æscet' meaning 'a collection of ash trees' or 'æscseat, a corner angle where ash trees grow'.

Hasted, quoting Lambarde, also tells us that the river ought not to be called the Stour until after it leaves Ashford, the original name for the stretch from the source at Lenham to Ashford being 'Eshet'. If this is so, then the name of the town clearly derives from a ford over that river. Many writers have followed Furley in stating that the ford which gave the town its name was the one at the bottom of East Hill, on the Hythe road. There was undoubtedly a ford at this point, but I do not believe that this is the relevant one. First

2.   *Trumpet bridge, on the Beaver road, at the beginning of this century. It is at this point that the ford which gave Ashford its name was situated.*

of all, if Hasted is correct, this ford is not on the Eshet at all—the two rivers which we call today the East and Great Stours originally joined approximately at the point occupied today by the main signal box off Newtown Road. Then, in Saxon times, all the lines of travel ran from the north-east to the south-west, as has been fully demonstrated by K. Witney in his *Jutish Forest*. The route from Ashford eastwards was of little importance, if it existed at all. There is a map of England dated about 1360, known as the 'Gough' map. The number of roads shown is very limited, but it does include a road leading from Sussex to Canterbury. For at least the last part, from Ashford onwards, this road follows the line of the Roman road. This confirms the view that this was the important road in early times, the road from Ashford to Hythe being of little significance until much later.

Lastly, anyone using the line of the Roman road would first cross the river by a ford near the present Beaver or Trumpet bridge, and would then find himself going parallel to the river. This would represent the 'corner angle' which is given as one possible original derivation of the name. So for these reasons, I consider that this ford is the one that gave the town its name.

Whatever the origins, there can be no doubt that Ashford was an established community by 1085, the year that King William the Conqueror ordered the making of the Domesday Survey. Like so many of the entries, that for Ashford is obscure. There are three references for Ashford: south Ashford (perhaps that area later called the manor of Licktop), East Stour (identified with the Domesday manor of Essella, and later called Esture), and to the town itself, where there was a church and two mills. It is clear that Ashford escaped any major destruction by William's soldiers after the battle of Hastings, since the total value of the three entries is given as 115 shillings in the time of King Edward (the Confessor), a small reduction to 95 shillings after the Conquest, and 150 shillings by 1086. This can be compared with Folkestone (where there was substantial destruction), which is given as having a value of £110 before the Conquest, only £60 immediately afterwards, and £100 in 1086. In addition to these manors that of Ripton (or Repton) is noted separately. Details of the entries are given in Appendix I.

2

The Manors

At the time of Domesday, Ashford was described as a manor, the fundamental method of organising land-holding that had originated several hundred years before the Conquest, but was shaped by the Normans to suit their concepts of land tenure and liabilities.

Under the feudal system, all land was deemed to belong to the king, all other persons holding some form of tenure from him, either directly or indirectly. Only the great barons (including high Church dignitaries) held directly from the king, being after the Conquest those who had accompanied William in the invasion, or had rendered him some great service. These important persons then granted tenures of part of their land to others, who might in turn repeat the process, this being known as 'sub-infeudation'.

Of course, the king (or lower lords who granted sub-tenures) expected some return for the use of the land. The most important of these was the responsibility to provide armed men to serve the king in times of war—this was the way in which medieval armies were recruited. Thus, for example, the king would grant certain lands to an individual who had to provide two knights (on horseback) and 20 foot soldiers. Instead of holding all the land himself the lord might grant the land to (say) two persons, each of whom would find one knight and 10 men.

In addition to land-holding by military service, other forms were possible. At the lowest level, where we are concerned with those men actually cultivating the soil, land would be granted on the basis that the man concerned would give part of his time to the working of the land retained by the lord to produce his own requirements of food. For the 300 years from the Conquest to the middle of the 14th century, much land was held in this way, the occupiers being under the absolute will of the lord as to when and for how long they worked for him. Such persons held land under a system called 'copyhold', since they had no deeds but merely had a copy of the court roll giving a description of the land and its abuttals and the details of when, and under what conditions, they were admitted as tenants of the manor.

From the 14th century this system began to decay, firstly because of the great labour shortage that occurred after the plague outbreaks of that century, and secondly because with changing practices it became more advantageous both to the lords and the tenants to change to a system of money-rents. Nevertheless, the legal entity of copyhold tenure continued until the beginning of this century, but with few real meanings. Writers from Lambarde in the 16th century onwards have stated that copyhold tenure was never widespread in Kent. The reasons for this are obscure, but the custom of gavelkind, which existed before the Norman Conquest, had a big influence. The most important part of this custom was that land descended to all sons equally (or in the absence of sons to all daughters), and not to the eldest (primogeniture) as in most of England. In earlier periods land could not be alienated by will to anyone other than those entitled under this custom, but gradually legal ways were found to circumvent this, and later power to leave land freely was given by statute. After that time the rule of gavelkind could only apply in cases of intestacy. Tenure

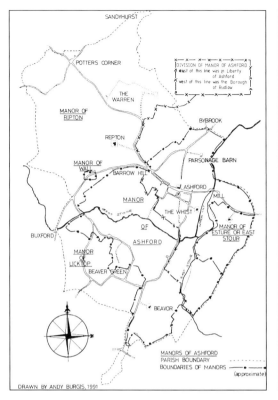

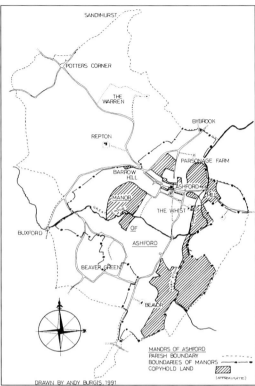

3. *Map of the parish of Ashford, showing the location of*
the several manors.

4. *Map of the manor of Ashford, with the extensive areas*
of copyhold land. Of special note are the large areas of meadow
adjoining the rivers.

described as copyhold certainly existed in Ashford over a substantial area, although I have been unable to discover any other manor in Kent where it existed for more than small pieces of land. The manor of Ashford continued its manor courts, and the practice of copyhold until the whole system was ended by the Law of Property Act of 1922.

Four manors are mentioned in Domesday, but by the 15th century the following existed within the parish:

Ashford manor—which included all the town area, north to Bybrook, east to the Willesborough boundary, to the south as far as Kingsnorth on the eastern side of Beaver Road, but only as far as Beaver Lane on the western side. On the west it extended as far as the Catholic church and the road to Tenterden.

Little and Great Ripton (or Repton)—which include the rest of the northern part of the parish.

East Stour—the area roughly of the railway works, and northwards towards Hythe Road.

Licktop—the area south of Beaver Lane but west of Beaver Road.

Wall—a small manor at Chart Leacon.

Some small areas within the parish are known to have been held of other more distant manors. Land just north of the lane leading from Potters Corner towards Godinton was held of the manor of Mardell, in Boughton Aluph, and a wood is named as Mardell wood in the tithe survey of 1843. When the first large scale Ordnance Survey map was published about 1870 the name was corrupted to Marble wood, and this error has been continued.

5. The Hare and Hounds *at Potters' corner has been a public house for many centuries. The premises were at one time part of the estate of the lord of the manor. The picture dates from the early years of this century.*

No maps exist showing the precise boundaries of these manors, and the descriptions of them only permit a general definition. Of these manors, only that of Ashford was of any size or value with appreciable urban development, the others being wholly agricultural land.

In 1086 Hugh de Montfort held the three Ashford manors from the king. He held East Stour himself, but granted the other two to Maino, of whom nothing is known. They remained in the Montfort family until *c.*1100 when Hugh's grandson, Robert, went on a pilgrimage to Jerusalem, leaving the manors to revert to the king. They were then granted to a family whose surname was merely 'de Ashford'. The first reference is to Norman who gave land in Ashford for the benefit of Horton Priory in 1142. In 1267 they were owned by Simon de Criol because he had married Maude, daughter and heir of William de Ashford. After the death of Simon, his widow married Roger de Rollyng and by 1271 they had sold the manors to Roger of Leybourne. The manor and advowson of Ashford, together with much other property, descended to Juliana of Leybourne, the great-granddaughter of Roger. Although she had a son by her first husband, John, 2nd Lord Hastings (Hasted is incorrect in stating that she had no children), Juliana had licence to hold the property personally, so that the property would not have passed to him on her death but would have reverted to the king. He would have been free to give the land to whomever he chose but, in order to prevent this, Juliana transferred all her property to trustees for the benefit of charitable purposes after her death. She died in 1367 and the manors reverted to the king for disposal in accordance with her wishes.

In 1382 King Richard II granted the manors of Ashford, Wall and East Stour towards the endowment of the Chapel of St Stephen in the King's Palace at Westminster, but in 1384 a grant was made to Sir Simon de Burley, a great favourite of the king and his queen, Anne of Bohemia. Simon supported the king in his struggle for absolute power and, in

6.   *The area immediately south of the river was low lying, and subject to flooding. Before the development that followed the opening of the railway works the land was valuable pasture, and annual flooding was welcomed as it encouraged a good growth of grazing. This picture is of Beaver road in 1907, when the flooding was not so welcome.*

March 1388, was impeached before Parliament. Found guilty on 5 May on a number of charges, he was sentenced to be hung, drawn and quartered, despite an appeal from the queen, who is said to have pleaded on her knees for Simon to pardoned. The king altered the sentence to beheading, which was carried out the same day. Later the same year the Dean and Chapter of St Stephen's Chapel were re-instated having been, in the words of the Close Roll, 'unlawfully thrust out by Sir Simon'.

The chapel continued in ownership until 1547. In that year the College of Canons was dissolved by King Edward VI, and the extensive property owned was surrendered to the king. In 1549 Ashford and East Stour were sold to Sir Anthony Aucher, of Otterden. Writing towards the end of the last century, Robert Furley claimed that he had found records that showed that the original sale by the Crown had been to Thomas Colepeper of Bedgebury, and that he had subsequently sold to Aucher. However, there does not seem any reason to doubt the entry in the Patent Rolls dated 29 August 1549 recording the payment by Aucher of £2,744 17s. 8½d. for the manors of Ashford and Esture and other property. Aucher mortgaged the property to Sir Andrew Judde but, as the mortgage could not be repaid, it became the property of Sir Andrew six years later. His daughter married Sir John Smythe of Westenhanger, and that family, created Viscount Strangford in 1628, continued in owner-ship until 1709. In that year they passed to Lord Teynham, who had married a daughter of Viscount Strangford. In 1765 the manors were sold to Francis Hender Foote of Bishopsbourne, and in 1805 his descendants sold to George Elwick Jemmett.

Members of this family had lived in or around Ashford for centuries. The first entry in the register is the baptism of Policarpus on 30 January 1585/6. This unusual name is probably taken from a saint, a Bishop of Smyrna about A.D.100, whose day is 26 January. This branch went to Wye, and I have not been able to discover if they were closely related to two Thomases who were in the town in the 17th century. One was a carpenter, and the other a maltster. At the end of that century there were two Daniels (father and son), both linen weavers.

The real involvement with Ashford begins with George and William, sons of Caleb Jemmett of Maidstone and his second wife Ann who was the daughter of Robert Elwick, vicar of Bredgar. 'Elwick' was used as the second name for five generations to preserve this link. The two brothers came to Ashford in about 1770. They or their descendants were not only lords of the manor, but also bankers, and were involved with much of the development of the town in the 19th century.

With the purchase of the manor in 1806, they acquired a large area of land, stretching from just below the churchyard to Beaver Lane. Amongst the houses that they owned was the large one on the site today of Lloyds Bank, the entrance to Bank Street being originally their garden. They developed the whole area including Bank Street and Elwick Road (named after the family, as was George Street, the name for the lower part of Bank Street until about 1880). They were fortunate to own much of the land south of the railway (which reached Ashford in 1842), and William, Francis and Bond Roads, as well as Jemmett Road are all named after members of the family. The last member of the family to live in the town was W.F.B. Jemmett, who was the last manager of Jemmetts' Bank, and the first of the branch of Lloyds with which the old bank was merged in 1902. The last member of the family was Maud, who died, unmarried, in 1951. Her legal representative retains the very limited manorial rights that remain—in practical terms only the title of lord of the manor.

One of the peculiarities of the manor, at least to modern thinking, was that, although it was a legal and judicial entity, it was not always a single geographical area. We have seen how the boundaries of the manor of Ashford differed from those of the parish, but there were also several quite separate areas that were part of the manor, and whose tenants had to appear in the *Court* in the same way as those who lived in the central area. This was particularly the case in Kent, derived from the farming practices of the Jutes. The main areas of settlement were in the north and west of the county, but during the autumn cattle and swine were driven into the forest of the Weald, to feed on the acorns and beech mast. Each manor controlled a specific clearing in the forest, called a 'denn'. In some instances the distance to be covered was quite considerable and, to break the journey, suitable staging posts would also belong to the manor.

Ashford manor included small pieces of land in the nearby parishes of Kennington, Willesborough, Sevington, Mersham and Aldington. Also part of the manor was the denn of Iborden in Biddenden.

The manor of Wall continued in the same ownerships until 1768, when it was sold to John Toke of Godinton, and by him to the Earl of Thanet. The occupation of land in this manor gave rights of pasturing animals on the common of Chart Leacon, and this led to a dispute in 1698. The steward of the manor of Ashford held a *Court*, and claimed to allocate these grazing rights. This was contested by the Earl of Thanet, who cited documents of 1445, when the manors had been owned by the Chapel of St Stephen, in support of his view that the two manors were quite distinct, and that a separate court should be held.

The manor of Ripton belonged in 1086 to the Abbot of St Augustine's Monastery at Canterbury, but by the early 12th century it was held by the family of Valoigns. After many generations, a daughter married Sir Francis Fogge, and this family continued to own the

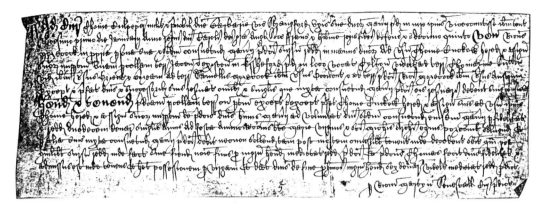

TO THE COURT of Thomas Culpeper, knight, and of the most noble Lady Barberia, Viscountess Strangford, his wife, Lords of the Manor, in right of the same Viscountess, held there on the twenty first day of January in the fifteenth year of the reign of the Lord Charles, [21 January 1640/1] by the grace of God King of England, Scotland, France and Ireland, Defender of the Faith etc., THERE CAME Richard Morecock in his own person, and according to the custom of the aforesaid Manor he yielded up into the hands of the Lords, to the use of Thomas Cuckow, his heirs and assigns for ever, one parcel of land lying and being in Ashford aforesaid, in a place called Tylton, namely to the land of Thomasina Sutton, widow, there towards the East and North, to the land of Samuel Morecock there towards the West, and to the land of the aforesaid Richard Morecock there towards the South; except and reserved to the aforesaid Lords and their successors all and singular those things which, according to the custom of the aforesaid Manor ought or are accustomed to them;

TO HAVE AND TO HOLD the aforesaid parcel of land, with the appurtenances, except as before excepted, to the aforesaid Thomas Cuckow, his heirs and assigns, to the use of the same Thomas, his heirs and assigns for ever, of the aforesaid Lords of the Manor at the will of the Lord according to the custom of the same Manor by fealty and the rent of twelve pence each year payable at the feasts of the Annunciation of the Blessed Virgin Mary and Saint Michael the Archangel by equal portions, and by the other services due according to the custom of the aforesaid Manor, and also paying, both after the death of each tenant dying seised thereof, and after each surrender thereof made or to be made, in the name of a fine for having entry, half of the aforesaid rent;

And the aforesaid Thomas did fealty to the Lords, and was admitted as tenant thereof;

And he has possession by the rod;

And he gives to the Lords as fine for having such entry six pence, namely half of the aforesaid rent,

By Richard Martyn, Steward of the aforesaid Court.

7. *The earliest known copy of the Court Roll of the Manor of Ashford, 21 January 1640/1, with translation of the original Latin.*

manor until 1596, when it was sold to Sir Michael Sondes. Five years later it was sold to John Tufton of Hothfield (created Earl of Thanet in 1628). Licktop belonged to the college of Wye until 1544 when it was sold by the king (after the dissolution of the college) to Sir John Fogge. This manor was subsequently in the same ownerships as Ripton. A detailed list of the owners of the manor of Ashford is given in Appendix II.

As well as being the owners of the land the owner of the manor, the lord, provided through the courts which he was empowered to hold, the only means of local government. These were of two types, Courts Baron dealing with the transfer of land from one tenant to another, and Courts Leet concerned with local administration and the prevention of nuisances. Courts were held every six months, and all the tenants were obliged to attend, and could be amerced (fined) if they did not appear. In the Ashford Courts, tenants were fined for non-attendance up to the 19th century—one shilling for copyholders or four pence for freeholders.

It was unusual for the lord to be present at the Court, especially in the Ashford manors, where no lord was resident in the area until the last century. The Court was held by an officer called the steward. These men obviously had considerable power in the community, being the rough equivalent of both the mayor and the town clerk of more modern local government. We know the names of the stewards from the 16th century, and they are also listed in Appendix II. The decisions of the Court were made by the homage, that is a number of freeholders acting as a jury.

By the 15th century, manor proceedings had become fixed by custom, and in many cases (including Ashford) we have a copy of these rules, written down and known as a 'Custumal'. These rules stated what the respective rights and obligations were. Nothing, not even the rents, could be changed. In time, because of inflation, the rents became not worth collecting, and in many manors the practice was abandoned—not so in Ashford where rents were collected right up to 1930 when they were abolished by law. The Ashford Custumal, agreed in 1516, is given in Appendix III.

The proceedings of the Courts were written on parchment, the sheets being made into rolls until 1814 then (in the case of Ashford) into books. For Ashford they still exist from 1678 for Courts Baron, and provide a great wealth of information of the owners and occupiers of land, and of family relationships. An idea of the change in the economic standing of tenants can often be learnt, since the mortgage of lands had to be declared in the Court.

The details of each transaction was copied on to a small slip of parchment, hence the term 'copyhold'. This was held by the tenant as the sole evidence of ownership of the land. The earliest example that has been found is dated 1640, and relates to a piece of land north of the upper High Street. The land is described as part of 'Tilton', the name of a very large field which was almost certainly originally an open field cultivated communally. The illustration shows this copy, with the translation from the original Latin. An example of the record of a session of the Court Baron for 1773, when the proceedings had become much more detailed, is given in Appendix IV.

In the case of Courts Leet, a similar procedure was followed. Unfortunately no rolls have survived, although Hasted states that these Courts were still being held for Ashford at the end of the 18th century. John Sills was a grocer in Ashford at the beginning of the 19th century, and his diary for 1809-21 has survived. He records attending meetings of the Court Leet and Court Baron on only two occasions, 12 October 1810 and 27 November 1811. On the latter occasion he tells how a dinner was given by George Jemmett (lord of the manor) in the *Saracen's Head*. After complaints by Jemmett of the quality of the wine they moved to the *George*, where Jemmett tried to persuade the whole company to get drunk—the dinner for those attending seems to have been the chief reason for attendance by this time!

Courts Leet were responsible for dealing with problems such as obstructions of the roads and overflowing cesspits. These powers were gradually taken over by the towns-people meeting in the Vestry in Easter week, when not only churchwardens were appointed, but also the surveyor of highways and, most importantly from the 16th century, the overseers of the poor. All of these will be dealt with more fully later.

In the first two or three centuries after the Norman Conquest, many manors had the right to the view of frankpledge. This was the recognition of all adult males in the community, who were jointly responsible for the keeping of the King's peace. Such manors also appointed annually a constable, an office known to have existed from Saxon times. By the end of the 13th century the constable had been established as the first link in the judicial system, leading upwards to the King's High Courts, and wishing to demonstrate clear authority, the Crown restricted the rights of manors: only those having a specific grant of the authority continued to have the right of frankpledge. The power to appoint constables passed to the Justices of the Peace.

It does not seem from the charters that the Chapel of St Stephen had these rights, and they were certainly not passed to the subsequent owners of the manor. Court Leet, how-ever, continued to nominate one of the residents as constable, and this choice was usually accepted by the justices, who made the official appointment. The justices made the appointment where the Court Leet either failed to nominate, or where the person chosen was unacceptable to the Justices.

Other Areas   As well as the manor, other divisions of land were established before the Norman Conquest and in some cases were continued for administrative purposes for many centuries afterwards.

Where the area of a manor was relatively large, a sub-division called a borough is found. This should not be confused with a town with a royal charter of incorporation, but was a small group of inhabitants separated from the main centre. Two existed in Ashford—the borough of Rudlow in south Ashford, and Henwood, on the eastern boundary on the road to Hythe. The land tax was collected separately for Rudlow borough, even in the 19th century, and the boundary is shown on the 1870 Ordnance Survey maps.

The hundred was greater in area than the manor. This unit had been established as early as the beginning of the 10th century in that part of England that was part of or controlled by Wessex. The hundred was both an area of taxation—the area assessed at a hundred hides of land—and of justice, with hundred courts settling disputes of a local nature. The hundred court elected a constable, who represented the hundred at shire courts. At the time of Domesday, the parish of Ashford was divided. The main manors were in the hundred of Longbridge (the crossing of the river on the road between Kennington and Willesborough) whilst Ripton was part of Chart hundred.

Among the rights and privileges granted to the Dean and Canons of St Stephen when they acquired the manor in the 14th century was that of being a liberty independent of the hundred for which a separate constable was appointed. Peculiarly, however, the area of the liberty did not correspond either with that of the manor or of the parish, since it did not include the northern part of the parish (largely the area of the manor of Ripton), nor the large part of south Ashford which was within the manor of Ashford but subject to the borough of Rudlow.

The loss of population and therefore of taxable resources to the liberty meant that the remainder of the separate hundreds were quite small, and they were merged to form the hundred of Chart and Longbridge in the first part of the 17th century.

The lathe was a division of the county peculiar to Kent, consisting of a number of hundreds, but possibly pre-dating them. It is thought that they may originally have been based on the areas of the estates of Jutish Kent, and that there were as many as a dozen. By the time of Domesday they had been reduced to five, with two further half lathes. Ashford formed part of the lathe of Wye.

During the 13th century there was a reorganisation in east Kent, with the number of lathes being reduced from five to three, and re-naming. Ashford became part of Scray lathe.

During the 17th century, changes of population again meant that the old divisions were becoming inequitable. The forced loan to Charles I was administered by commissioners, and a separate commission was appointed for the hundreds 'annexed to the lathe of Shepway' (broadly corresponding to the modern district of that name). These hundreds were those of Chart, Calehill, Nether and Upper Wye, Felborough, and Longbridge, and the township of Ashford. By the end of that century these areas had been permanently transferred to Shepway. Hasted, writing at the end of the 18th century, describes them as 'long since separated from Scray'. Like the hundred the lathes were used for the definition of legal or taxation areas until the last century, but had little other significance.

3

The Church

―――――――――

We know from Domesday that there was a church in Ashford in 1086, quite certainly on the same site as today. The ministers are known from 1282 and are listed in Appendix V.

We do not know who was responsible for the building of the first church, but the Domesday Monachorum (a record compiled by the monks of Canterbury *c*.1100) lists Ashford church as dependent on Wye.

In the beginning the persons who had caused the church to be built would have had the right to appoint the minister, and this was usually in the hands of the lord of the manor. Before many centuries had passed, however, this right, technically called the 'advowson' and which could be a valuable one if the church was richly endowed, became separated, and could be bought and sold like any other possession. Pearman states that in the 12th century, Norman de Ashford granted the advowson to Horton Priory, but it seems that it later reverted to the manor since it certainly belonged to Juliana of Leybourne. After her death the king gave the advowson of Ashford to Leeds Priory, and this continued until the

8. A view of Ashford church from the north-west, early in the last century.

9. (above)   The church from the south, in 1868.

10.   A view of Ashford church from the north-west, taken in 1972. A comparison with no.8 shows the extent of the widening of the church about 1830.

dissolution. Henry VIII then gave it to the Dean and Chapter of Rochester Cathedral. The Ecclesiastical Commissioners are the owners today.

It is not the purpose of this book to give a detailed account of the structure of the church. The building has been adapted throughout the ages to suit the needs of the population, and Pearman gives much information based on the examination by several distinguished architects. He states that the fabric shows traces of Norman, Early English, Decorated and Perpendicular construction. To which we may add the later Victorian and 20th-century improvements.

The main body of the existing church is in the Decorated style of about 1250. There is evidence of partial rebuilding perhaps towards the end of the 14th century, but the general appearance as we know it today dates from about 1475. It was then that Sir John Fogge, of Repton, and a prominent politician in the time of the Wars of the Roses, renovated the church and built the bell tower.

Substantial alterations to the building were made in 1827. In that year the aisles of the nave were widened in order to accommodate a growing congregation, and a new entrance door on the north side was constructed. A further extension was made in 1860, when the church was lengthened towards the west, providing 230 additional sittings.

The political and religious controversies during the 17th century caused many upheavals. The impact on individuals is discussed in chapter 5, but changes were made in the interior of the church of Ashford at this time.

Ashford had acquired a reputation as one of the centres of non-conformity in East Kent—described by one writer as 'the most factious in all Kent'. A substantial number, probably a majority, of the inhabitants supported non-conformist views, including the churchwardens. In 1644 they were responsible for removing the altar and altar rails. They then had a stone with their names placed in the wall of the church to commemorate their work.

It was not until 1695 that steps were taken to reverse these changes. In that year the altar was rebuilt, and the stone removed from

11.   The priory of Horton (near Sellindge) was founded by Robert de Ver about 1155 for Cluniac monks. The church and land in Ashford was given to the Priory for its support. Since the dissolution of the priory by Henry VIII the buildings have been used as a private dwelling, and the picture shows them today, much altered internally but retaining the character of the original.

the wall. The cost was met by subscriptions totalling over £70. Full details of the subscriptions, and of the statement describing the events are given in Warren.

New pews were provided in 1745, of the tall closed box variety. These were replaced in 1879 by the present open seating. The first gallery was built in 1616, and a second (for the boys of the grammar school) in 1637. The side galleries date from 1717/8. The west gallery, used to contain the organ, was erected in 1772.

An inventory of church goods taken about 1550 shows that there were then six bells. These were replaced in the 17th century, and two more added in 1762 (again by subscription), so that the tower now contains eight bells. Apart from their use for services and on special occasions, the bells were rung daily in the morning and at night. At the beginning of the 18th century the sexton was paid £4 16s. 0d. a year for ringing the waking bell at four and five o'clock in the morning, and at eight and nine o'clock in the evening, and for other duties. In 1816 a set of chimes was installed to play tunes, both religious and secular. Made by John Apsley of Ashford, they first played on 4 June—the King's birthday. A new set was provided in 1885, with a different repertoire. It is not known when the practice of ringing a 'waking bell' at 4 or 5 a.m. was discontinued, but Pearman states that the ringing of a curfew at 8 p.m. in winter and 9 p.m. in summer, followed by a 'day of the month bell', was discontinued in 1889.

In 1464, at the request of Sir John Fogge, the king granted a licence for the establishment at Ashford of a college of priests. Unfortunately the king, Edward IV, died before the

The Souldiers in their passage to York turn unto reformers pull down Popish pictures, break down rayles, turn altars into Tables,

12.   During the Commonwealth period many churches, including Ashford, were altered to accord with puritan beliefs. This illustration (not of Ashford) is typical of the times. In Ashford the changes were strongly supported by the churchwardens, Joy Starr and William Worsley, who had a stone cut with their names and placed in the east wall. (by courtesy of the Ashmolean Museum, Oxford).

legal procedures for this college could be completed. Fogge at first was not in favour with the new king, Richard III (although they were reconciled later), and so the college was never constituted with perpetual succession.

Since the college had never been legally constituted, it did not require legal procedures for its dissolution. In 1550 John Ponet, then vicar, was licensed to give away the lands with which the college had been endowed. Without the income from these lands the priests to serve the college could not be paid, and so it ceased. Despite this the house in the churchyard continues to be known as the College, although used as the vicarage.

Fuller details of the church can be found in: the manuscript written by William Warren—a curate and son of the vicar—in 1712, and printed at the end of the last century; Pearman's *History of Ashford*; *Ashford Church* by Charles Igglesden, in several editions from 1901; *An Illustrated Guide to Ashford Parish Church* by W. Burden (1989).

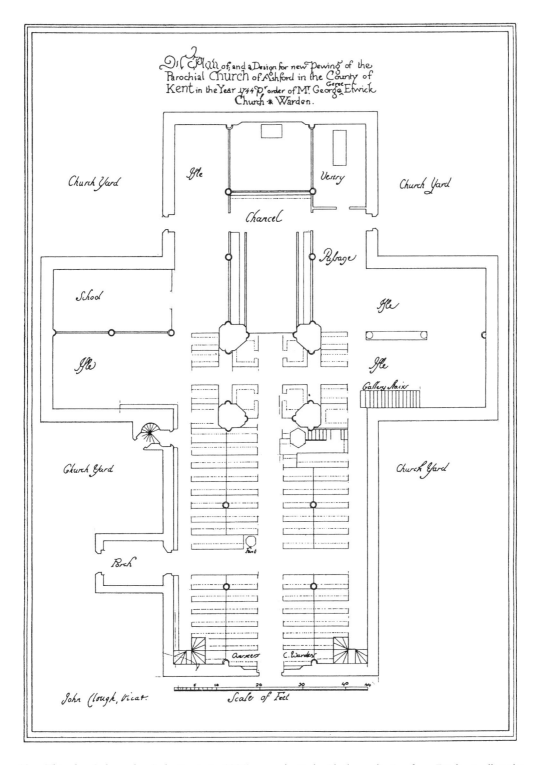

13. *This plan (redrawn by Andy Burgis in 1991) was submitted with the application for a Faculty to allow the erection of new pews in Ashford church in 1744. Note the area set aside for a school.*

4

Town Life in the Late Medieval Period

By the beginning of the 13th century, Ashford was established as the market centre for the surrounding area. The oldest buildings are those clustered around the churchyard and the market area, now the High Street. This was originally much wider and less obstructed than it is now. The central blocks that we know today as Middle Row were not built until about 1500, and the frontage on the south side of the lower High Street was further back. It is probable that this market area was on the fringe of the town, with open fields extending down to the river.

Firm evidence for the growing importance of Ashford as a market is in the three charters that were granted between 1243 and 1466 to the lords of the manor. The first was granted to Simon de Criol and his wife, Maud, by Henry III. It allowed a weekly market on Saturdays, and an annual fair on the 'eve, day, and morrow of the Decollation [beheading] of St John the Baptist', 28, 29 and 30 August.

In 1348 another charter was given to William de Clynton, Earl of Huntington, and his wife Juliana (of Leybourne). This gave authority for another annual fair, to be held on 'the vigil, day and morrow of St Anne', 25, 26 and 27 July.

Lastly, in 1466 the Dean and Canons of the Chapel of St Stephen in Westminster were granted an annual fair on the 'vigil and day of the St John before the Latin Gate, and the two days next following', 5-8 May. The text of these charters (a translation from the original Latin) is given in Appendix VI.

The Dean and Canons of St Stephen were most important and influential lords. They, above all others, had the capital and access to expert advice in the management of their estates. Walter Briscall has shown (Arch. Cant. vol.CI, p.57) that 1 Middle Row, the building facing down the High Street, was the original market house, from where the market could be controlled and tolls collected. The original structure dates from before the ownership of the manor by St Stephen's Chapel, but it was considerably improved by them.

It is also likely that they were responsible for the alteration and improvement of the river. As was said in chapter 1, the two rivers originally joined at a point higher upstream than today. At some time a new artificial cut was made, to create the stretch on the western side, shown on today's maps as the Great Stour. As late as the 19th century, this was shown on maps as the Lord's cut. It was made to improve and regulate the flow of water to the mill at the bottom of East Hill. This must be the site of the mill mentioned in Domesday, and it belonged to the lord of the manor until 1805. No documentary evidence has been found as to the precise date when this cut was made, but it is likely that the new channel was cut during the last part of the 15th century. The improvement was certainly made before 1562 since the records of the Sewer Commissioners (responsible for control of rivers) exist from that date, and they make no mention of the cut being made.

This period was one of great unrest in this country. The 14th century had seen the social upheaval caused by the Black Death in 1348-49 but this was by no means the only occasion when plague was prevalent. The population had been rising steadily since the Norman conquest, and was possibly as high in 1340 as it was to be at any time in the next 400 years. This led to pressure on resources, especially food production. All available land was used for cultivation, including much that was of poor quality. Woods were felled and marshes drained. This situation was completely reversed by the plague outbreaks in the second half of the 14th century, because at least one half, and in some areas a greater proportion, of the population died. From being a land with an excess of labour, workers became scarce. In some manors the shortage was so great that the lords (or more likely their stewards) attempted to attract labour from elsewhere, despite the laws and customs that bound copyholders to their manors. Higher wages were offered, and to combat this Parliament passed several laws, such as the Statute of Labourers, in an attempt to hold down wage rates (in which they were generally successful), and to keep down prices (which was less successful). Not surprisingly, many labourers resented this control, and this together with the imposition of a poll tax resulted in the Peasants' Revolt of 1381, led by Wat Tyler. No names are known of Ashford men who took part in the uprising, but there are records of violence as close as Boughton Aluph and Wye. In the enquiry that was held afterwards it was alleged that houses at both places were plundered and documents burnt, and amongst those charged were John Henwode and Stephen Repton—both names having Ashford connotations.

In the next century, conflict at national level led to the Wars of the Roses, between the rival claims to the throne by the Yorkists and the Lancastrians. Many Kent families were involved, and in particular Sir John Fogge, of Ripton. He was present at most of the battles, and had a personal interest since his second wife was a cousin of Elizabeth Woodville, wife of King Edward IV. Fogge was Treasurer of the Household of this King. Fogge fought at the battles of Northampton, St Albans and Towton. Undoubtedly tenants of Fogge at Ripton would have been required to accompany him to battle, but again no names are known. When Richard III came to the throne in 1483 Fogge lost his lands, and was probably lucky not to have been executed. He was pardoned, and within a year his lands were restored to him.

The uprising of 1450 associated with the name of Jack Cade seems to have originated in Ashford, or in its immediate neighbourhood. Cade adopted the name of John Mortimer, but was also known as the 'captain'. The records of the town of Lydd include a payment of fourpence for a horse for the constable to ride to Ashford 'to aspye tythynges of the Captaine of the [H]Oste'. Unlike the Peasants' Revolt, that of Cade was supported extensively by respectable middle-class gentry. Opposition in Kent was against the royal officials, who, it was said, were oppressive and abused their powers, but no doubt there were other reasons for some of those who joined the revolt. Foremost amongst the officials were William Crowmer, sheriff of Kent and his father-in-law, Lord Say and Sele, treasurer of England, both of whom were killed by the rebels when they captured them in London. Although at first well disciplined, the rebels grew over confident and out of hand. They then lost the support of London. Offered pardon by the king, most of them accepted, and dispersed. Cade was pursued and finally captured and killed. Whether this took place at Hothfield near Ashford, or Heathfield in Sussex seems impossible to determine with certainty.

In Shakespeare's play *Henry VI, Part 2* there is a character called Dick, the butcher of Ashford. He clearly had no time for the legal profession, whose influence was held to be against the common people. In discussing what they should do after their rising had been successful, he declared 'first thing, let's kill all the lawyers'! Unfortunately for Dick (and the

14.   The view looking down East Hill, probably taken about 1930. Until the opening of the by-pass in 1957 this was part of the main road from London to Folkestone and Dover.

others), the rising did not succeed, but many of those involved were pardoned, including seven men from Ashford. The only butcher in this list is William Egerynden, and the only Richard a man called Burman, a chapman.

There was another uprising in 1471, when Thomas Fauconberg, natural son of Sir William Nevill, landed at Dover from Calais, and then marched to London intending to release Henry VI from his imprisonment in the Tower. Before he could do this he heard that Henry had died, so he withdrew, finally surrendering at Sandwich. Sir John Fogge took part in the march, and was among those who received a pardon from King Edward IV afterwards.

Despite all these troubles, life went on for the townspeople. From the middle of the 15th century we know more about them—their names, and those of members of their families, and of their occupations and trades. The more prosperous made wills which are still available, and much information can be found in them. By the standards of today, their possessions were very few, but they were concerned to ensure that they went to the persons they chose. The wills also show concern for the well-being of other people. At a time when the provision of public services was minimal, money was left to repair roads—thus William Deen gave 10 shillings in 1476 to 'repair the bad road between my messuage and Gore Hill', Richard Bacon left '5 marks to repair bad roads between Ashford and Kyngesnorth' in 1479. Rising standards can be seen in the concern for the education of children—Henry Cosyn in 1476 directed that his son 'Robert be found scole while he can write and read'. Donations were made to the parish church for improvements, such as William White, who gave 40 shillings in 1473 towards the new work of the rood-loft. This, no doubt, was work being carried out at the time the church was remodelled and the tower was added by Sir

John Fogge. Most frequent were gifts of money to pay for candles to be lit before the images of the various saints, as the 12d. given by John Sandyr in 1461 for the light of St Anne, on whose day one of the markets was held.

The battle of Bosworth in 1485 was the end of the struggle between the rival factions for the Crown, and with the crowning of Henry VII England became less of a battle-field. The growing controversy was over religious matters. This had begun as early as the 13th century with the teachings of John Wyclif. His views on the need for some separation between the church and the state received much popular support, and he and his associates were responsible for the first publication of the Bible in English. During the following century there was sporadic support for his views, although the state and the church used harsh methods to suppress them. Throughout the 14th century men and women were brought before church courts accused of heresy, among whom were one from Willesborough and many from the Tenterden area. Those inspired by the teach-ings of Wyclif were termed 'Lollards', and this description was used in the following centuries to describe those expressing views contrary to those of the catholic church. The popular anti-clericalism was a contributory factor in the rising of Jack Cade.

15.   *That part of Hempstead Street from the junction with High Street to that with Tufton Street was one of the town's oldest routes, leading to Hempsted wood. Until the nineteenth century it was called Drum lane, the house on the corner with New rents being an inn called the Drum. This view was taken in 1972, but apart from the road surface and the yellow lines, has much the same appearance as would have been the case for at least the previous two hundred years.*

The religious arguments, interwoven with opposing views of differing political factions, dominated the scene for the next 200 years. Ashford was to become very much involved in these arguments, which are discussed more fully in the next chapter.

5

Religion and War
in the 16th and 17th Centuries

As was said at the end of the last chapter, the 15th century ended with growing religious controversy.

The persecution of those thought to be Lollards or heretics increased, and attempts were made to obtain confessions from those accused, the critical point being the doctrine of transubstantiation. The years 1511-12 saw particularly strong action, led by the Archbishop of Canterbury, William Warham. In May 1511 a large number of persons from east Kent were brought before him at his palace at Knole, including John Brown, a cutler of Ashford. The general atmosphere can been appreciated by the statements of Joan Harwood of Rolvenden, who was questioned at the same time. She said that she, her husband Thomas and Brown had discussed their beliefs 'sitting by the fire in the hall'. It was agreed by them that they would never tell others of their beliefs as it would 'cost them all their lyves to be brent and it were uttered'.

John Brown was burnt on Whitsaturday, 30 May 1517. The execution took place in Ashford, either in the High Street or in a field by Ashford Bridge. This field was certainly used later for the same purpose, and was known as 'martyrs' field' afterwards. Richard, son of John Brown, was imprisoned at Canterbury in 1558 and was sentenced to die, but was saved by the death of Queen Mary before the sentence was carried out.

This is not the place to go into the detail of the quarrel between Henry VIII and the Pope over the divorce of Catherine of Aragon, and the establishment of Henry as the sole head of the Church of England, but there can be little doubt as to where the sympathies of many Ashfordians lay. Apart from the early instances already mentioned, the views must have been influenced by the vicars of the parish, such as John Ponet, vicar from 1547 to 1551. Pearman says that he was a skilled mathematician, and that he presented Henry VIII with a clock showing not only the hours, but the days and the change of the moon. He had a great ability as a preacher, and was appointed first as Bishop of Rochester, and then in 1551 to Winchester. As a strong Protestant he was clearly not in sympathy with Mary, the catholic queen who succeeded her brother Edward VI in 1553.

In 1554 Sir Thomas Wyatt, of Allington, led an attempt to overthrow Mary. He was supported by many men from Kent, including Sir John Fogge (grandson of the one who had rebuilt Ashford church). Ponet was in London at that time, waiting and hoping for the success of Wyatt. When it became apparent that this was not to be, Ponet, with others who shared his views, fled to Strasbourg, where he died in 1556.

Although laws against heresy, providing for death by burning, had been passed by Parliament as early as 1400, the numbers executed had been relatively small. The years 1554 to 1558 are those that led to Mary being termed 'bloody'. During these years at least 288 persons, men, women and children, are known to have been burnt alive as heretics, 54 of them in Kent. It was usual for the executions to take place away from the home town of those condemned, in order to reduce the possibility of friends and supporters trying to release the prisoners. Thus two men from Tenterden, Nicholas Final and Matthew Bradbridge, were burnt at Ashford on 16 January 1557. Their widows suffered the same fate at Canterbury on 19 June following.

Five Ashford men are known to have been burnt, all at Canterbury. The first was Humphrey Middleton on 12 July 1555, then Richard Wright, William Stere and Richard Colliar, all on 23 August 1558. The last was John Herst on 11 November in the same year. As stated above only the death of Queen Mary, on 17 November 1558, saved Richard Brown.

These events ceased with the death of Mary and the accession of Elizabeth (although trials and executions of both Catholics and Anabaptists continued on a much smaller scale), but the personal bitterness between individuals must have continued. In 1570 William Padnall, who was the bailiff to the manor of Ashford, was charged with seditious words. Edward Fogge gave evidence that he said to Padnall 'thowe arte a papiste, and was a papiste in queen Mary's dayes', to which Padnall was alleged to have answered, 'I care not for queen Mary or for queen Elizabeth, and for anything that I have done in either of their tymes, I am able to answer'. Unfortunately the record of the Assize Court in which the case was heard is damaged, and we cannot know for certain the verdict. However, since Padnall continued as bailiff until he died in 1584, it is to be assumed that he was acquitted— perhaps bound over to keep the peace.

By the second half of the century puritan belief amongst members of the Church of England and the beginnings of non-conformity were to be found in Kent, particularly in the towns. To combat this Archbishop Matthew Parker, archbishop of Canterbury, issued rules for the conduct of services, but these were widely ignored. In 1581 Joseph Mynge, a puritan, was appointed vicar of Ashford. He was one of those clergy who refused to subscribe to the six articles of Archbishop John Whitgift in 1583. These were intended to enforce compliance with the views of the church of England, and Mynge would no doubt have been punished by the church courts for his views, had he not died in May 1584.

In the 17th century many town corporations, or groups of parishioners appointed 'lecturers' to preach and discuss church doctrines to as wide an audience as possible, in many cases in opposition to the views of the local minister. Thomas Brewer was appointed in Ashford sometime before 1626, but in that year he was prosecuted and imprisoned. In 1629 Alexander Udney was appointed to Ashford, but he was removed in 1630 and in 1631 appointed vicar of Folkestone. A report of the examination of the circumstances by archbishop Abbott reads:

> the vicar of Ashford, Edmund Hayes, is reported to have the outside of a man and little more; for ignorance he has sufficient for any one person; for indiscretion enough for the clergy of a whole diocese; and thereby running into contempt of his people, who being about about 800 communicants, most of them understanding men well read in the scriptures, desired to have assigned to them some learned conformable man, who might teach them the way to heaven, they paying their minister all his dues and entertaining a lecturer or co-adjutor.

On 15 January 1632 it was agreed by the parishioners that the vicar, together with those of Hastingleigh, Charing, Elham, Hinxhill, Wye and Kennington should be asked to give a lecture weekly on Saturday afternoons. This arrangement was confirmed in December

1634, when it was agreed that John Roberts, the parish clerk, should seek contributions to pay for these lectures. In 1642/3 Parliament approved a request from the inhabitants of Ashford that Joseph Boden should be apppointed to give a lecture on Saturday mornings and Sunday afternoons. He became vicar the following year.

There were many supporters of puritanism in the Wealden cloth towns such as Tenterden and Cranbrook, but by 1600 some had moved to Ashford. The religious views of these people had much in common with those of Dutch and Huguenot families who came to England at about this time. They came to escape from the persecution in their own country, and obviously found sympathetic support in Ashford. Under Charles I they had the same concern for their continued religious freedom as had the Pilgrim Fathers, who left for New England in 1630, and many decided to take a similar action. Research has shown that of 197 people who are known to have gone to New England from Kent between 1620 and 1650 no less than 17 were from Ashford. One group was under the leadership of Comfort Starr of Ashford, a surgeon, son of Thomas Starr a hosier who came to the town from Cranbrook about 1600. They sailed from Sandwich in the ship *Hercules* in 1636. Other members of the Starr family followed, including a son, also called Comfort. He was one of the first scholars at the University of Harvard, and later, as a member of the staff, was one of the signatories of the founding charter.

In 1633 William Laud was appointed Archbishop of Canterbury, and he was emphatic in believing in the need for uniformity and adherence to the formal procedures of the established religion. He had, however, little tact, and his insistence on being treated with great pomp led to great unpopularity with those of more puritanical views. In 1637 he was writing 'at and about Ashford the Separatists continue to hold their conventicles, notwithstanding the excommunication of so many of them as have been discovered. They are all of the poorer sort, and are very simple'. The ring leaders were Thomas Brewer, John Fenner and John Turner, who had been imprisoned. Laud was concerned with other matters—he also complained that there was a butcher's slaughterhouse opened in the churchyard in Ashford. Despite Laud's complaint, it remained for another 300 years!

Charles I came to the throne in 1625, determined to rule according to his personal views on the correct doctrine of the Church of England, and of the rights and duties of the people.

One aspect of this was a renewed attempt to enforce attendance of everybody at church on Sundays, and Acts requiring this were passed in 1625 and 1627. Edward Berwyn of Ashford was charged at Quarter Sessions that 'being over the age of sixteen years he did not repair to the parish church of Ashford between December 1629 and January 1630[/31]'. The overriding need of Charles was to raise revenue. Taxation was agreed in 1625, but growing criticism led to the dissolution of this first Parliament, as well as a second called in 1626. An attempt to raise revenue by means of a forced loan (without Parliamentary approval) met with little success, and Charles was obliged to call another Parliament in 1629. On this occasion religious differences as well as the question of taxation were the issues. After the Commons had passed a resolution against the possible introduction of catholic practices and the levying of taxation without Parliamentary approval, Charles again dissolved Parliament. He now hoped that he would be able to raise income without the need to summon Parliament. Many savings were made in the cost of the Court and of other services, but these alone were insufficient. It was decided to enforce the payment of 'ship money', an old form of tax previously levied on coastal areas to defray the cost of defence. The levy in 1634 was in accordance with this rule, but in subsequent years the writs demanding payment were issued to all parts of the country. This aroused great objection, and the refusal of John Hampden in Buckinghamshire to pay led to a test case, which Hampden narrowly lost.

It seems that there were Ashfordians who were no more enthusiastic! In January 1638/9 the King's Council issued a warrant for Thomas Cuckow, constable of Ashford, to appear before them to explain why payments were £17 in arrears. On this occasion he sent a memorandum promising to assist in the collection, but this was apparently of limited success, since in May a second warrant was issued. Ten days later, on 17 May, Cuckow appeared, again promised to assist, and was discharged. He was an unlucky man—in 1650 he was charged by the Parliamentary County Committee with being a delinquent—a supporter of the Royalists. Although the case was disproved, his estates were seized, and in 1651 he was asking for details of the charges against him. He petitioned the Committee for Compounding that 'he was charged with being in the late Kent insurrection: having a very small estate prefers to compound rather than appeal'. He paid a fine of £54 6s. 8d., one-sixth of £326. The effects of this action were not confined to Cuckow. In June 1651 Henry Spicer, a lad of 17, petitioned in respect of a mortgage to Cuckow by his grandfather, also Henry Spicer. The land involved had been given to the grandson, but was seized by the County Committee as part of the estate of Cuckow.

In 1642 the gentlemen of Kent submitted a petition asking for certain rights and privileges to be granted by the king. Their general view was in support of the monarchy, but against the extreme actions taken by Charles. Substantial landowners, such as Toke at Godinton and Tufton at Hothfield, were generally supporters of the Royalist cause, or moderate Parliamentarians. Ashford, and many other towns in Kent, adopted a more radical attitude. In 1643 the vicar of Ashford, John Maccuby, was ejected and replaced by Joseph Boden. He was a presbyterian, and later preached to the County Committee. He is said to have taken down stained-glass windows in the College, and at this time the old altar in the parish church was destroyed by the churchwardens, Joy Starr and William Worsley. They had a stone carved with their names and the details, and this was placed in the wall of the church. It was removed in 1695, when a fund was raised to provide a new altar. Joy (or Joyful, to give him his full name) was the brother of Comfort Starr who emigrated to America in 1636.

With the return to the monarchy of Charles II in 1660 an Act of Uniformity was passed, to which all parish ministers had to subscribe. Those who were unwilling, like Nicholas Prigg of Ashford, another presbyterian vicar (who had replaced Boden in 1647), were ejected, but he continued in secret as the minister of the independent or congregational church. He may have been the person to whom reference is made in a letter to Henry Bennet, secretary of state in 1663: '70 persons were arrested at a private house in Canterbury, and I have sent to Ashford to take a preacher'. Later the same year, it was reported that the people were dissatisfied with new taxes, and that there were two baptist ministers at Ashford.

There was limited religious freedom at this time, but very few records have survived of the position in Ashford. Many different non-conformist sects were started, one of which was supported in Ashford. A report to the government was made in 1667 that 'at Ashford and other places we find a new sort of heretic after the name of Muggleton, a London tailor, in number 30'. Some muggletonians, as the sect was called, certainly lived in Ashford, and were openly acknowledged. The church registers record the burial of Robert Davis and Francis Baker in 1680, and Matthew Davis in 1684, all described as 'muggletonians'.

The Compton census of 1676, which purported to give accurate figures for the number of non-conformists, gives only 80 in Ashford, out of a population of about one thousand. This would appear to be a gross understatement, since there is clear evidence of a greater number of dissenters. This is borne out by the fact that in 1688 Ashford was anxious for the early departure of James II, and the arrival of the Prince of Orange. Sir John Knatchbull of Mersham recorded in his diary that on 8 December he 'went to Ashford ... [and] sent for the Chief of the Town and told him ... that it was very hazardous to us and the Prince's cause to declare for him out of season, and prayed them earnestly to be quiet and endeavour to keep the people so'. A few days later Lord Salisbury and Sir Edward Hales had been captured (at Ashford by the 'mobile' or 'rabble' according to the diary of Sir John, but this seems a doubtful authority). The confusion did not last long. On Christmas Day 1688 James landed in France, never to return. Sir John Knatchbull reported that by the end of the month he had secured many signatures of support for William, including those for Ashford.

With the accession of William III and Mary, the legal restrictions on worship by non-conformist congregations came to an end, although the Test Acts prevented non-anglicans (catholics and non-conformists alike) from holding public office. Both independent (congregational) and baptist churches were openly established in Ashford, and continue today. A list of their ministers is given in Appendix V. Fuller details of the non-conformists in Ashford can be seen in *History of Religious Dissent in Ashford* by A.C. Watson.

With its long history of non-conformity it is not surprising that there are no references to catholicism in the 18th century. The newcomers working in the railway works from 1847 brought members of the church to Ashford and in 1857 the Reverend Edward Sheridan hired a room for services at 111 New Street, which had been a private school. Ironically this building later became a public house, named the *Prince of Orange*, the protestant William III invited to England to oust the catholic James II. Subsequently services were held at a number of addresses, but about 1861 (under the leadership of Reverend Anthony Oromi) permanent sites were considered. The first to be purchased was in North Street, but this proved to be too small, and was sold. The site at Barrow Hill was purchased, and a new church, designed by Edward Pugin was opened on 22 August 1865. Various alterations and extensions were made in subsequent years, but the whole has now been demolished and larger premises built.

16. *The Catholic church at Barrow Hill, opened in 1865, and demolished and replaced by a new building in 1990.*

The concern of the established church about the number of non-conformists in Ashford can be seen in the application to the Consistory Court in 1716 for permission to erect a new gallery in the church when it was stated in support 'a great number of the Inhabitants have not room and convenient places to kneel, stand, sit and hear divine Service there read and celebrated, the which it is justly feared will as it is manifest it hath already done by the number of the Inhabitants now frequenting the Presbyterian, Independent and other Meetings'.

One matter which continued to cause controversy was the payment of tithes. Originating in biblical times, or even earlier, this was the payment of one-tenth of the increase in value derived from crops or livestock, and with the income derived from lands donated to the church, were the support of parish clergy.

Where, as in Ashford, the rectory or advowson became separated from the vicarage, there was a division of tithes. 'Great tithes', derived from crops of corn, hay, wood and so on, were payable to the rector, whilst 'small tithes' were left to the vicar. Originally tithes were paid in kind, but from as early as the 15th century arrangements were made in some areas for a money payment to be made instead. Tithes were predominantly a payment from agriculture, since none were due from houses or other property in towns. There were also a number of exemptions such as forests.

The system seems to have been accepted and to have worked reasonably well until the 17th century. The growth of non-conformism led to opposition from those who saw no reason to pay towards the upkeep of a church whose views they did not share. They had, of course, to pay for the establishment of their own chapels and ministers in addition to the payment of tithe.

After the civil war, attempts were made by many of the clergy to enforce the payment of tithes. They considered that many payments that had formerly been due had not been re-instated, or only paid at a lower level. The parish register for Ashford records in 1678 'that in the years 1674 & 1675 the wood commonly called Lodge Wood, lying in the parish of Ashford belonging to the Earl of Thanet, was felled and Tithe was paid to me Samuel Warren: vicar.There was a tryall about it at Maidstone Assizes in the year 1677 in Lent'. An entry records that, in 1681, 12 cords of wood were paid as tithe in kind, but in 1684 £2 15s. 0d. as composition was paid when further felling took place.

In Kent much controversy was caused over the question of tithes on hops. They were a new crop, introduced in the first half of the 16th century, for which no ancient custom existed. They were also a valuable crop, so that the amount of tithe involved justified action by the church to enforce payment, and by occupiers of land to contest the claims. Disputes concerned not only the principle of payment but also the methods; for example, should the tithe be each tenth hill or plant (but yields might vary from plant to plant), or every tenth row (but rows varied in length), or one-tenth of the picked hops? The scope for argument was considerable.

In 1631 Thomas Starr was the 'farmer' of the rectorial tithes—he had taken a lease from the Dean and Chapter of Rochester Cathedral, and was entitled to collect the tithes from the occupiers. He took action in the Church Court against Thomas Cuckow who had eight acres of land which had been converted to a hop garden, and on which he had refused to pay tithe. However, there seems to have been personal animosity as well, since at the same time Cuckow was alleging that he had been libelled by Starr. Evidence was given that, whilst they were standing in the High Street, Starr had called Cuckow 'a base drunken fellow'. Religious beliefs were also involved—Starr was a puritan (and later emigrated to America), whilst Cuckow was charged with being a Royalist in 1650.

The arguments over the liability for tithes on hops continued. In 1670 the vicar of Ashford, Thomas Risden, attempted to recover tithes due from Thomas Crouch that had lapsed during the Commonwealth. The case resulted in actions in both the court of the

King's Bench and in the Exchequer of Pleas to determine whether hops were great or small tithes. Much opposition to the payment of tithes came from the Society of Friends, the Quakers. There were members of the Society in Ashford from the mid–17th century (when they were formed) and in the 18th century the records show several Ashford persons refusing to pay. In 1781 pewter belonging to Joseph Blundell, a cider maker of New Street, and valued at £1 12s. 0d. was taken by Order of the Justices. Richard Marsh had four sheep taken in 1781, and wheat and oats in 1784.

Opposition continued throughout the 18th century, and eventually, after several failed attempts, a revised system was approved by Parliament in 1836 by the Tithe Commutation Act. This Act required that Commissioners should have surveys made for each parish. The surveys consist of a map, with every field shown, and with a reference number. A schedule was then made for each field giving the reference number, the names of the owner and occupier, the area, the name or description and the state of cultivation—pasture, arable and so on. The average total of tithes that had been paid for the years 1829-35 was then apportioned to each field on the basis of area. The amounts found by these calculations were converted to a 'rent charge' by reference to the amounts of wheat, barley and oats that could be bought for £100 in 1836. These amounts were revised annually to reflect the changes in price of those crops.

By and large, the new system was accepted, and controversy was reduced. It was not entirely eliminated. Arguments arose when land was sold in small parcels, as for example when a field was used for housing development. Opposition in principle also continued and flared from time to time. As late as the general election of 1929 tithes were an issue in rural areas. Small farmers had been hard hit by the depression, and felt that the payment of tithes was an unfair burden. The liberal candidate for the Ashford division in the Parliamentary election of 1929 was Rev. Roderick Kenward. The reform of the law in respect of tithes was a major issue, and against all expectations he gained the seat. He was defeated in the next elections two years later. There is a small memorial to him in the field on the north side of the A20 opposite Yonsea Farm, near Potters Corner.

Following the report of a Royal Commission, the rent charges were replaced in 1936 by a tithe annuity that was to be payable for 60 years, after which the whole system would cease. Inflation since the war has reduced the value of the fixed payments to such an extent that in the vast majority of cases the annuities have been extinguished by the payment of a lump sum.

6

Population and Health

For several centuries after the Norman Conquest we can have only the vaguest idea of the population of Ashford. If national trends were reflected then there may have been as many as 1,000 inhabitants by the middle of the 14th century, with a substantial drop in the following years due to several outbreaks of plague and other diseases.

By the middle of the 16th century, the population of England was rising again. From this time, too, we begin to have some idea of the population trends, because of the introduction of parish registers. In 1538 Thomas Cromwell had ordered the keeping of books with details of all persons baptised, married or buried. At first these books were of paper, but it was realised quite quickly that they would not have the permanence that was desired. In 1595 orders were issued that from that time parchment books were to be used, and the entries copied from the old books, at least from the accession of Queen Elizabeth in 1558. According to the statistics collected with the census for 1831, nearly one quarter of all parishes have registers from before 1558, but unfortunately those for Ashford do not start until 1570.

From the summary of the numbers in each decade from 1570 to 1800 (just before the first census of 1801) we can get some impression of the gradual increase in population. This is, however, far from a complete picture since it ignores the numbers of persons moving in or out of the town. These are particularly important since Ashford seems always to have been a place of changing population. Family names prominent in the records for one century generally disappear in the next, and new names appear. The best estimate that can be made suggests that from perhaps seven or eight hundred in the 16th century, the population rose to around 1,200 at the end of the 17th century.

In 1662 Parliament passed a law to allow a new tax, replacing some of those of Charles I that had been so unpopular and were abolished. The new tax on hearths was to cause even more controversy, in particular because it empowered local constables to enter houses in order to check the number of hearths declared by the householder.

The tax was abolished in 1689, by one of the first Acts of William and Mary, being described in the preamble as 'whereas the revenue of Hearth Money has been grievous to the People, not only a great oppression to the Poorer sort, but a Badge of slavery on the whole people, by exposing houses to be entered into and searched'.

The Act has, however, left one benefit to historians, the schedules of collections that were prepared by the constables. These exist for 1664 for the whole of Kent, and show not only the number of hearths and the amount paid, but also the names of all the occupiers. Those for Ashford show 268 premises, with a further 21 in the borough of Rudlow which was assessed separately. Of these 116 were exempt on the grounds of the poverty of the occupant. If it is assumed that the average household was of four and a half persons, the population of Ashford was about 1,300 at this time. It is unfortunate that after the first years the collection of the tax was 'farmed', that is sold to a contractor for a fixed sum, leaving him to collect as much as he could. The records of these farmers have not survived, thereby depriving us today of a record that would have given much information about the inhabitants over several decades.

There is one other indication of the population in the first part of the 18th century. When the churchwardens applied to the Consistory Court of Canterbury for permission to erect a gallery in the church they stated as the reason 'the parish of Ashford is very large and populous consisting of sixteen, fifteen, fourteen, thirteen or at least twelve hundred souls'. The arguments of the churchwardens in order to get support for the proposal may have rested on doubtful arithmetic, but the statement clearly supports the calculation made from the earlier hearth tax.

In line with the national figures, there was probably a slight fall in the first half of the 18th century, but with a sustained increase from about 1760. By 1801, the date of the census and the first time an accurate figure is available, the population was 2,151. Thereafter the increase was rapid, as can also be seen in the summary in Appendix VII, reaching 12,808 by 1901. This increase to six times is far greater than the increase for the total population of England and Wales, which only increased by three and a half times in the same period. The reason for this was the establishment of the railway works, discussed in more detail later.

The burial registers give us some idea of the incidence of disease over the centuries. If the number of burials in any year is more than twice the average for the decade, it can be assumed that some form of epidemic occurred. For Ashford this happened in 1578, 1584, 1594, 1625, 1687, and 1741. In 1625 this was due to an outbreak of plague, some 100 persons being marked in the register as dying from this disease. The situation was so bad that the Justices levied a special tax on the neighbourhood to relieve those without means of support, or, as they phrased it, 'lest the sick should be forced for the succour of their lives to break forth of the town to the great danger of the country'. In 1741 the deaths were almost certainly due to smallpox, since, although the registers give no indication, several cases are recorded in other documents at about this time. Thus Matthew Thurston made a verbal will in April of that year 'before dying of smallpox', as did William Chexfield in July. Susan Reader said in her will of 1717 that she wished 'to be buried at Bredgar unless I die of smallpox'. She was buried at Ashford in 1732, so it is presumed that she did die of that disease, which was greatly feared in this century. Despite some success with inoculation with live serum, it killed many people, but some escaped. John Adcock made his will in December 1740, and was described as 'sick in body', but he recovered, not to die until 1756.

The treatment available for those who were ill must have been very limited. The earliest known surgeon is John Busse, who died in 1547, and the first physician John Tilly, licensed in 1574. In the early part of the next century there were immigrant Dutch doctors, such as Lodowicke Rowzee who died in 1639. Others were John Jacob Vanderslaert and Israel Vanderslaert, perhaps brothers. It seems possible that Amos Jacob, a physician who lived at Barrow Hill and died in 1688, was the grandson of John Jacob, having adopted the second name as his surname. This would explain the cryptic entry in the register of the burial in 1664 of 'Mr Jacob's father'—the Dutch name being beyond the capability of the parish clerk!

There is no record of any form of hospital provision until the 18th century. No doubt alarmed by the outbreaks of smallpox, the parish officers used a farm on the very boundary of the parish (part in fact in Kingsnorth) as a 'pest house'. This property, near Clockhouse at Beaver, was known as 'pest house farm' as late as 1840 when the tithe survey was made, although it had long since ceased to be used for that purpose.

17 & 18.   Two views of the Cottage hospital in Wellesley Road. It was erected by 1877 with money donated by Mr William Pomfret Burra in memory of his wife.

At the beginning of the next century, prevention rather than cure was introduced. The parish arranged for poor persons to be vaccinated against smallpox, using the new vaccine introduced by Edward Jenner.

Provision of accommodation for treatment of other illnesses did not come until the middle of the 19th century. A group of public-minded individuals were responsible for starting a subscription list which resulted in the first hospital in Station Road, at no. 20/22, on the site that had been occupied by the gas-works until then. This opened on 1 January 1870 with 14 beds and was called St John's House. A report in the *Kentish Express* recorded gratitude to Sir Edward Hoare, Mr. Charles Pemberton Carter and especially to Mr. John Furley. The latter had been very active, and the newspaper credited him with the conception of the idea, and a large share of the work of raising funds and planning. This building was replaced by the cottage hospital in Wellesley Road, which opened in 1877. This was paid for by William Pomfret Burra in memory of his first wife, Isabella Nottidge, at a cost of £3,000, excluding the value of the site. In 1928 the new hospital in King's Avenue replaced this hospital.

The isolation hospital at the Warren was built in 1860 as a private venture, being paid for by Henry Whitfeld, a surgeon in the town. In 1876 it was leased by the Local Board for 21 years at £20 a year. The Board extended the premises to provide an isolation hospital, for the treatment of cases of cholera, smallpox, etc. It was closed in the 1970s.

It is not surprising that Ashford has one of the earliest Corps of the St John Ambulance Association, since John (later Sir John) Furley was born in 1836 at 32 North Street (where there is now a commemorative plaque). He was one of those involved in the formation (in 1877) of the Association, the main object being the teaching of first aid. The first Corps to be founded was at Margate (in 1879), but this later seceded from the national body, leaving the Ashford Corps (founded in the same year) as the oldest existing today. The present headquarters are in Maidstone Road, in the appropriately named 'Furley Hall'. Furley also developed a litter and stretcher, to be used for the conveyance of patients. This was built locally, called the 'Ashford litter', and was the standard equipment used by the Association for many years.

Details of later developments are given in chapter 14.

7

The Poor

Writing in the 19th century Disraeli, in his novel *Sybil*, said, 'Two nations; between whom there is no intercourse and no sympathy; who are as ignorant of each other's ways, habits, thoughts, and feelings, as if they were dwellers in different zones, or inhabitants of different planets; who are formed by a different breeding, are fed by a different food, are ordered by different manners, and are not governed by the same laws ... the rich and the poor'.

This difference perhaps reached its peak in the first part of the 19th century, but its origins are much older than this. The uprisings of the 14th and 15th centuries were supported by the landless labourers hoping to improve their lot, although they were led by those whose economic position was somewhat better. The need for governmental institutions to make provision for the poor in the time of Henry VIII is popularly ascribed to the abolition of the monasteries. There is no doubt that this was a factor, since many of those institutions had given relief to poor persons, but increasing population, poor harvests and the return of soldiers from continental wars were the underlying economic reasons. As a result of these factors, added to which was the debasement of the currency by the Tudor sovereigns, there was considerable inflation—grain prices increased by about six times between 1500 and 1600, and the purchasing power of the labourers' wages was halved.

During the 16th century Parliament passed laws that were to govern the principles of poor relief for the next 300 years. In 1536 the churchwardens were required to collect voluntary contributions from parishioners for poor relief, and in 1547 weekly collections were to be made after exhortation by the preacher. At the same time it was enacted that cottages should be built for the poor, and relief given to them. Further legislation required those who did not contribute to be reported to the bishop, and if they still did not respond, they could be imprisoned. Under an Act of 1576 towns were to gather stocks of wool, etc., to provide work for the poor, and those refusing could be imprisoned.

Despite all this legislation, there is very little record of action, and none traced for Ashford. In 1597 a new Act introduced a compulsory system, with the levy of a poor rate. Two officers called the overseers of the poor were to be appointed by the parish at a meeting held in the vestry in Easter week. With the two churchwardens they had the power and responsibility of providing relief for the poor, and levying rates on all occupiers of property in order to meet their expenditure. In 1601 all these Acts were repealed and re-enacted. The rating principles of this Act, usually referred to as the Statute of Elizabeth, remained as the basis of local government finance until the introduction of the community charge in 1990.

An important feature of the poor relief system was that each parish was responsible for its own inhabitants. Over the following centuries this principle led to everyone having a legal place of settlement, and much distress and hardship was caused by its enforcement. As early as 1616 the Ashford overseers were concerned to have the following recorded in the register, after the entry for the baptism of Isaake, the base born son of Elizabeth Hanes, late of the parish of Westwell.

> MEMO: that on October 19, 1616 Sir Nicholas Eylborne, Sir Anthony Dearing, and Sir Isaake Sidly did agree uppon an order & willed it to be recorded in the register that although the foresaide Isaake was to be baptised here, yet the parish of Esheforde sholde not be charged with it if hereafter it proved vagrant.

The problem that concerned the administrators at that time (as it does many people today) is how they could distinguish between those who were ill or old, and therefore deserving of relief without question, and those who could be expected to maintain themselves, if they had work. In order to cater for the latter, many parishes provided a 'stock'— materials and perhaps tools which could be made available to those without work or any capital with which they could start. The more affluent parishioners would often leave sums of money in their will for poor relief, and in some cases money for the provision of a stock. Thus in his will dated 1625 Thomas Milles left £200 for stock for the poor of Ashford. There is some doubt as to what happened to this money, since in 1677 the parish went to law, claiming that it had not been paid. The money was secured on property previously owned by Milles, but which in 1677 belonged to Sir Thomas Twisden. A Commission was set up to enquire into the matter and, meeting at Sittingbourne, it decided that the money had been paid to the parish many years earlier.

After the restoration of the monarchy the regulations governing settlement were tightened. By an Act of Parliament in 1662 the justices were given the power to authorise the compulsory removal of paupers whose place of settlement was elsewhere. The laws governing the acquisition and change of the place of settlement were complex, and in the succeeding century gave rise to much litigation.

At this time changed ideas were introduced to deal with the problem. Despite the failure of a workhouse system in the previous century, it was re-introduced in some areas. Instead of giving an allowance in cash to the poor, to enable them to pay their rent or to buy essential food, institutional relief was provided. Ashford was very early in this move. In 1705 the parish acquired premises for a workhouse, and petitioned the Justices to be allowed a keeper. They agreed, and William Luckett was appointed. He died in 1717, and there is no record of when his immediate successor was appointed.

There was at this time no general statutory power or encouragement for the provision of workhouses. This did not come until 1723, when a bill was introduced into Parliament by Sir Edward Knatchbull, one of the members for Kent. Since he lived at Mersham, he must have known of the Ashford workhouse, and have considered the scheme worthwhile.

In 1729 the Justices agreed that the premises in Ashford should be used not only as a workhouse, but also as 'a house of correction for the close keeping and punishing of disorderly persons and incorrigible rogues'. This was not a great success, since in 1732 John Rufford, who was then the keeper, was charged with permitting several prisoners to go without the permission of the Justices. He was discharged, and the Justices decided that the premises were no longer to be used as a prison.

Controversy and discussion about the best methods of dealing with the problem of the poor increased during the 18th century. There were the fundamental differences between those who considered that the problem would be lessened by harsh treatment, and those who adopted a more generous attitude in the belief that the condition was beyond the control of the individual. In 1770 John Toke of Godinton, who was a justice and sheriff of the county in that year, wrote a number of letters setting out his views. Whether they were originally written to individuals, or subsequently published in this form is not known, but they take the form of advice to the parish officers of an unnamed place. Rules for the conduct of the workhouse, and for determining who should and who should not be admitted are set out at length. The views expressed were adopted virtually in their entirety by the Ashford parish authorities.

We are fortunate that the minute book of the Vestry meetings from 1757 has survived, and from that we can learn a great deal of the proceedings. William and Mary Smithson were appointed in May 1757 as keepers of the workhouse, at 6s. a week but, in addition to this 'in-relief', payments were being made to meet the rent of cottages or to buy provisions and clothing. In December 1770, it was decided to adopt new regulations based on the views of John Toke. These rules were amended in 1786, and both are set out in Appendix VIII. It will be seen that they include items relating to the general government of the town as well as those strictly relating to the workhouse.

A committee was appointed each year to supervise the administration of poor relief, and appears to have worked satisfactorily until 1785. In that year it was necessary to appoint a new keeper of the workhouse, as William Lyon, who had replaced Smithson in 1782, died. There had been changes to make the conditions more like a prison in 1770 (when a cage and stocks were erected) and in 1781 when the garden was enclosed by a brick wall. There was clearly a wish in 1785 on the part of some ratepayers to introduce an even more severe regime. The prime mover was Henry Creed, a draper, occupying the premises on the corner of High Street and North Street. He recommended as workhouse keeper John Pasmare of Marylebone, at £20 a year plus 10 per cent of the earnings of the poor. Pasmare was required to visit Cheshunt, Hertfordshire, to enquire of their methods of employing the poor. His proposals included the walling of the ground adjoining the workhouse, and the appointment of an attendant whose duties were to include the preventing of the poor from going out without leave. New rules were proposed for the workhouse and, although they were adopted by the Vestry meeting, there was opposition from at least one member. Thomas Waterman wrote in the minute book: 'seen and disapproved of every particular part of this Plan, and think Mr Creed an unfit person to have anything to do with the Parish of Ashford'.

Another change at this period was the introduction of paid officers. It was clearly found that the volume of work was beyond that which could be expected to be carried out efficiently by unpaid 'volunteers'. In 1777 the parish voted £5 5s. 0d. to Mr. Richard Bayly for his trouble in assisting the overseers, and further sums were voted in subsequent years. In this change too, Ashford was in advance of the general practice. General power to pay overseers was not authorised by Parliament until an Act of 1818.

The strict interpretation of the laws of settlement led to ever increasing expenditure on enforcement. At birth a child acquired the settlement of its father, unless illegitimate when the parish of birth was relevant. This led parish officers to try to get unmarried expectant mothers moved to another area if possible. The settlement at birth remained unless certain events took place. For example a man could acquire another settlement if he rented property of more than £10 a year in value, or if he was apprenticed or employed in another parish on a contract for at least one year. A woman acquired a new settlement on these conditions, but also on marriage she took the settlement of her husband.

The administrative procedure was that a parish, when required to give relief to someone it considered belonged to another parish, would apply to a justice of the peace for an order for removal. That parish in many cases would appeal to Quarter Sessions, and a decision would be given either to uphold or quash the Order. If still not satisfied with the decision, further appeal could be made to the High Court. Apart from the costs involved in obtaining and contesting orders, if removal was upheld costs would be incurred in the actual removal. There could also be considerable hardship for the family, particularly where there were children from more than one father in a family. This could arise not only where the wife had a child before marriage, but also in the case of children of a previous marriage. The settlement of the older children would continue to be that of their father (if legitimate), or otherwise of their place of birth. They could, therefore, be removed to a different place to that of their mother, whose settlement was that of her current husband.

The lengths to which Ashford was prepared to go in order to limit its expenditure can be seen from the following examples:

1. In 1634 the parish obtained a licence for marriage of Edward Parker and Mary Kipping, 'he having got her with child, and now under the custody of the constable'. The register shows that this was not the first child of Mary, so it is to be assumed that the parish had seized on Edward to limit their future liabilities.

2. In 1729 Ashford appealed against an Order of the Justices for the removal of Isaac Holland, his wife and family from Ickham to Ashford. The order was confirmed in respect of Isaac, his wife and the younger children, but it was found that the eldest had been born before the marriage of the parents. As a bastard this child had settlement in its place of birth, and so the order was quashed in respect of this child, which would have remained at Ickham when the rest of the family were returned to Ashford.

3. Relatives of a pauper could be required to contribute towards their upkeep. In 1748 it was reported that 'Thomas Grant of Ashford, grandson of Thomas Grant, yeoman, is a poor impotent person, not able to work, and is become chargeable to the parish. The grandfather is of sufficient ability to relieve and maintain him, and therefore Ordered to pay 3/0d per week to the Churchwardens and Overseers'.

4. In 1754 John Johncock was charged by the parish of Ashford with running away and leaving his family chargeable to the parish.

5. In 1774 Mary Dodd was charged 'as a loose, idle, and disorderly Person, lying at her own Hands [i.e. unmarried and not a minor] and refusing to Work, and thereby becoming chargeable to the Parish of Ashford'. She was sentenced to hard labour for one month.

6. In July 1775 Richard Taylor was charged on the oath of Elizabeth Waters, single woman, 'with having gotten her with child which is likely to be chargeable to the parish of Ashford'. Since Taylor was unable to find suitable sureties he was committed to prison until the next Sessions. He was discharged in October 1775. There is no record of the baptism of a child in the Ashford registers, so it is likely that the child was stillborn, and the imprisonment was unnecessary.

7. Perhaps the parish was more justified in taking action in 1794 against William Pearson, charged at the same court with being the father of the children of Grace Honey and Mary Wraight! As usual in these cases, the father was ordered to pay 2s. 0d. a week and the mother 9d., as long as the child was chargeable to the parish. In the case of more prosperous fathers a single payment of £10 was accepted, in settlement of all claims by the parish.

8. Even potential liability was a concern. In 1771 the *Castle Inn* had been leased to John Ivy, who came from Great Chart, at a rent of £8 a year. This was below the limit for acquiring a settlement in Ashford, but Ivy had taken the brewing house and equipment at an extra £4 a year. Counsel's opinion was sought as to whether the rent should be taken as £12, thus giving Ivy legal settlement in Ashford. Ivy died in March 1775 and his widow remarried with John Wilson. She (and her subsequent children) took the settlement of Wilson, but the three children of Ivy kept his settlement. There is no evidence that there was any immediate likelihood of the children being in need of relief, but the parish was prepared to spend on legal costs in order to be sure of its position if it ever happened. Counsel's opinion was that the payments should be taken together, an opinion that must have disappointed the Overseers.

Towards the end of the 18th century reform of the poor law became the subject of considerable political debate. Because of the effects of the Napoleonic wars and several years of bad harvest, the amounts being spent on poor relief rose considerably. For Ashford the total in 1776 was £772, but by 1813 had risen to £2,105. This increase of 173 per cent was less than that for the whole of Kent, for which the increase was 297 per cent. This was slightly smaller than that for the whole of England and Wales, for which the increase was 321 per cent. This fact alone was the cause of great alarm to the comparatively small proportion of the population who paid for this relief, by way of the poor rate. Other causes of dissatisfaction were the inability of amateur, unpaid overseers to deal effectively with the administration (particularly in those areas where the population was increasing rapidly because of industrial development), and the substantial expenditure being incurred in legal expenses.

Two Acts of Parliament were passed on the initiative of William Sturges Bourne, member for Christchurch and later for Bandon. The first has already been referred to—that passed in 1818 to allow the appointment of paid overseers. In the following year a further Act made a more radical change. This provided for the replacement of the 'open' vestry, where all ratepayers could attend and vote, by a 'select' vestry with the voting power of an individual being increased if he occupied property with a larger rateable value. This system was adopted in Ashford in 1820.

The great interest in reform led to a number of inquiries and reports being prepared. Some were made at the instigation of Parliament, but others were undertaken by individuals. One such was by Sir Frederick Eden, whose report after a visit to Ashford in 1795 includes information on the general trade of the town as well as poor law matters. He details the arrangements for the running of the workhouse (in accordance with the rules adopted in 1786), and says that about sixty persons were living there. They were employed in a bleachery, recently established for the bleaching of linen. This was in St Johns Lane, and was owned by Robert Houghton. Eden also reported that 'poverty here is attributed to the low price of wages and the high price of provisions'. This would seem to be self-evident, but he did qualify his comment by 'they suit each other in summer, but not in winter'.

Eden also said 'that the poor in Kent 10 years ago always ate meat daily, but that now they seldom taste it in winter, except in the poor house. Their usual diet is tea, barley or oat bread, potatoes and cheese'. By 1830 there was a growing belief that a change in the poor law was necessary. It was realised that one of the greatest difficulties was the very large number of separate parishes, mostly very small. In 1831 it was stated that there were about 15,500 parishes, of which more than 12,000 had a population of less than eight hundred.

An attempt had been made earlier to encourage voluntary amalgamation, particularly in 1781 when an Act of Parliament (Gilbert's Act) was passed. This had relatively little effect, and none in the area of Ashford.

Parliament finally decided that reform was necessary, and appointed a Poor Law Commission to make enquiries and recommendations. In 1834 an assistant commissioner, Ashurst Majendie, visited Ashford, and was impressed by the efficient running (in his eyes) of parish affairs by the select vestry. They had been able to reduce the expenditure on poor relief very substantially, but it is doubtful whether this enthusiasm would have been shared by those whose relief had been curtailed. The report by Majendie is given in Appendix IX. At about the same time, a report appeared in the *Quarterly Review*. This gave a verbatim report of a weekly meeting of the select vestry, at which applications for relief were considered. It is too long to reproduce here, but is to be found in Volume 53, pages 513/17. It opens with these words: 'the system of administering relief to the poor in the parish and town of Ashford is so creditable to East Kent, it has produced such beneficial effects, and it offers such valuable instruction to the Poor Law Commissioners, as well as to the country in general, that it may be useful to lay before our readers a short account of it'.

Further details of the conditions in the Ashford workhouse can be learnt from the select vestry minute book. Thus in June 1833 they resolved that 'Mr Elliott [the workhouse master] be ordered to keep the men apart in the house from the women, to prevent the increase of paupers'. This was not acceptable to James Head, who on 26 December 1833 threatened to leave his wife and children on the parish, if he were not allowed to sleep with his wife. Permission for him to leave the workhouse (with his family) was refused, and on 1 January it was reported that he had not been to work for several days, was drunk, and abusive to several vestry men. He was taken before a magistrate, who seems to have had more sympathy, since on 22 January it was recorded that Head should leave the house, and a parish house made available to him and his family.

There was further trouble in October 1834, when George Newton was drunk when he returned to the workhouse at 10 p.m. He was ordered to be confined in the cage for 24 hours on bread and water. It was also ordered that if any inmate returned drunk, he or she was to be put in 'the black hole' till sober!

In 1834 Parliament passed the Poor Law Amendment Act, based on the principle of 'less eligibility'—that conditions in the workhouse should be worse than those obtainable by a labourer on the lowest wages, and that no outdoor relief should be given to the able bodied. By these means it was hoped that all those who were capable of work would do so. In this it was no doubt successful: until 1929 when the system was finally abolished there was a real fear on the part of many old people of 'being sent to the workhouse'.

The big administrative change in the new law was that the liability of the parish as the unit was abolished in favour of unions of adjoining parishes. In the Ashford area two areas were created—East and West Ashford. They comprised the same areas that became the two rural districts under the reform of local government in 1894, and were only abolished in the latest changes of 1974. The administration of the poor law was supervised by a body called 'board of guardians', whose members were elected by the ratepayers, with the addition of the justices of the peace, *ex officio*. The West Ashford Guardians met for the first time on 6 June 1835, in the *Saracen's Head*, Ashford. An assistant commissioner, Sir Francis Head (appointed Governor of Canada in November 1836), was present and Rev. Nicholas Toke was appointed chairman. It was agreed that future meetings would be held weekly in the *Thanet Arms*, Hothfield.

No doubt as a result of the favourable reports made by the commissioners on the way that Ashford was run, it was not at first included in the area of either union. This did not prove acceptable to the parish, and they applied to become part of the West Ashford Union. This was agreed and became operative from 25 April 1836. Two additional guardians (William Walter of the *Saracen's Head* and Mark Dorman, leather seller) were elected to represent the interests of the town. This change meant that the existing workhouse and other property was not required. Ashford proposed that the buildings be used for housing the poor, at no rent. This was opposed by the Poor Law Commission, it being stated that 'this amounts to almshouses, and would be injurious to the poor'. The property was eventually sold for a total of £603.

The most important concern of the new guardians was to build a new workhouse to replace the parish buildings. The West Ashford Guardians decided on a site at Hothfield and, after several attempts to find suitable land, one acre, one rood and eight perches were purchased from George E. Sayer for £260. The contract price from Messrs. John & Thomas Allen of Maidstone was £3,770, but changes in the plans resulted in the addition of £1,637 or 42 per cent—the problem with public works costing much more than the original estimate is obviously nothing new! The total cost for the building, land and costs was £5,900.

Despite very strict control by the Commission, the West Ashford Guardians seem to have acted in a relatively generous way, but not to able-bodied persons. They reported in 1836 that they were not supporting any able-bodied paupers, although there were 241 such persons receiving relief before the new system was introduced. They continued to pay out-relief, although to fewer persons. In the first few months they accepted a tender from William Morley, a grocer of Ashford, for double Gloucester cheese (at £2 18s. 6d. a hundredweight), but later changed this for the cheaper single Gloucester. On several occasions in the first years of their administration they applied for permission to pay out-relief or to take into the workhouse children of able-bodied men, contrary to the rules of the Commissioners. Thus in April 1839 they took into the workhouse a child of John Burbridge of Smarden. His family consisted of himself, wife and six children, and his average earnings were said to have been less than 8s. 0d. a week during the previous six weeks.

In general West Ashford seem to have acted with more consideration for the poor than the Guardians for East Ashford. In the annual report for 1836 their Chairman stated, 'I think the industrious labourers are well aware that the idle can no longer impose and gain support as before, and are therefore more contented and are themselves thus benefited, not having to pay rates for keeping them, and are more attentive and civil ... a beerhouse in Wye parish was closed within one week after relief was given to the paupers in kind, nor has it been opened since. The receipts of most, if not all others have materially fallen off. The bastardy regulations have proved a very important check to the birth of illegitimate children, as the new laws have been to improvident marriages. I learn that only two marriages took place last Michaelmas at Ashford, when hitherto there have usually been eight or ten'. The source of this information is not known, but it is not true of Ashford parish church—there were no marriages in September 1832, 1834 or 1836, and only one in 1831 and 1833. In 1835 there were three.

West Ashford Guardians made early provision for the schooling of children in the workhouse. From August 1836 a schoolmaster or mistress was apppointed (sometimes both). On the other hand admission to the workhouse was virtual imprisonment, inmates being allowed only limited time outside. In July 1836 the Guardians resolved that 'permission be granted to the inmates of the Workhouse to walk out of the same at certain periods in the day, with leave of the Governor'. In November 1839 this was defined more precisely as 'aged inmates be permitted to leave the workhouse for two hours three times per week in winter'.

One new development was the encouragement (and financial contribution to the costs) of paupers to emigrate, both to Australia and to Canada. On the other hand 'involuntary emigration' added to their difficulties—in 1846 the workhouse held the families of three men convicted at Ashford Petty Sessions, and transported to Australia, a total of three women and 11 children. On other matters, the Guardians acted much like their predecessors. They pursued claims against the putative fathers of illegitimate children, and advertised for information on those who had abandoned their families—in the *Kent Herald* for April 1840, 'Robert Steed, late of Ashford, aged 26, 5ft. 8in., dark brown hair, large grey eyes and swarthy complexion has absconded and left his wife and family chargeable to the parish. Reward of £2 for information'.

The administration of relief for the poor was continued by the Guardians until the passing of the Local Government Act, 1929. The powers were then transferred to the County Council, which was responsible until taken over by central government by the provisions of the National Assistance Act of 1948.

8

Education and Charities

Mention was made earlier of instances where individuals left instructions in their wills for the education of their children. Unfortunately nothing is known of the schooling facilities that existed in Ashford before the late 16th century.

Teachers required the licence of the Church, and in many cases were the lesser clergy, since much of the earliest teaching was intended to enable townspeople to be able to understand and read the Bible, and to help in church services. Others seem to have combined teaching with other occupations. The first licence known to have been issued for Ashford was that granted to Samuel Cranmer M.A. in 1579. Four years later a licence was issued to a John Robins who, if not a teacher in the sense accepted today, was certainly literate, since his signature appears as the witness to many wills of this period. If he was, however, the same man who made his own will and died in April 1621, his main occupation was that of innkeeper!

About the end of the 16th century a 'petty school' (for young children) was established in the town by Thomas March. He claimed to have 16 pupils, probably including John Wallis, son of the vicar of the same name. He was undoubtedly the greatest scholar born in Ashford, and was a pupil locally until 1625. Because of the plague in that year, he was then sent (at the age of nine years) to a private school near Tenterden for further education.

March died in 1629, and thereafter a school was run by Thomas Beven until his death in 1657. In 1647 Unton, Lady Dering wrote to Henry Oxinden,

> I have spoken with with Mr Beven of Ashford concerning your daughters being with him [at school] ... he is a conscienable, discreet man ... so industrious for the benefiting of his scholars ... he will spare no pains to bring them to perfection ... besides the qualities of music both for the virginals and singing and writing and to cast accounts, he will be careful also that their behaviour be modest and such as becomes their quality . ... his wife is an excellent woman, and his daughter a civil, well qualified maid ... I presume you will think £30 a year for both [daughters] reasonable.

The major advance was made about 1635, when Ashford Grammar School was founded, due to the generosity of Sir Norton Knatchbull, of Mersham Hatch. Unfortunately he died before the formalities could be completed, but his nephew and heir, also Norton Knatchbull, honoured the wishes of his uncle. He transferred to trustees 32 acres of land at Newchurch, and charged this land with the payment of £30 each year for the upkeep of the school.

Detailed regulations were set out in 1638 for the governing of the school. These included the appointment of the governors, and the subjects to be taught. Entrants were required to be able to read and write, which would not only have restricted those coming to the school to the children of the more prosperous inhabitants, but also pre-supposes the existence of other schools where these subjects were taught. The first master of the grammar school was Baptist Piggott. Details of him and of his successors are given in Appendix X.

The school expanded and gained a good reputation in the succeeding years, reaching its peak perhaps in the second half of the 18th century, particularly under the headship of Stephen Barrett. In 1767 Barrett joined with others to ensure that adequate accommodation for the master and boarding pupils was available. A house in the High Street (on the site of 73 High Street) and one behind (which adjoined the schoolroom) was conveyed to trustees. The school continued to prosper until about 1850. The census of 1851 records that there were 36 scholars living in the school house, including some from abroad. There were also the head, his wife and nine children and two ushers, so they must have been quite crowded.

From that time, however, it began to decline for reasons which are not very clear. The population was increasing rapidly with the building of the railway works, and one might have expected the school to grow even bigger. This did not happen, and the school closed in the summer of 1871. The old school, the schoolhouse in the High Street and the adjoining land used as a playground were sold. The money realised from the sale, together with other donations, was used to build a new school in Hythe Road, and the foundation stone was laid in August 1878. This building was used until the school was transferred to new adjoining premises in 1958.

Other schools to teach the more basic skills of reading, writing and arithmetic must have existed throughout the 18th century, but there is virtually no record of them. A school was held in the church, since in his manuscript history William Warren writes of 'the wall where the Writing-master Teaches School', and the plan of the church in 1744 (when the new pews were installed) clearly shows the area used as a school. Later there was a school at the back of buildings in the upper High Street and Castle Street, as the will of Thomas Matson of 1769 leaves his 'building, previously a shop, now a schoolhouse' to his son John. In 1789 these premises were acquired by Elizabeth Smyth, a schoolmistress. At her death in 1800 the premises passed to her brother-in-law, Rev. William Disney, vicar of Pluckley, and then to his widow, Anna Maria, until 1820.

By 1790 there was established the 'Ashford Academy', of which the principal was James Alderson. Alderson lived at first in the lower High Street (on the south side), but by 1793 he had purchased premises in Hempstead Street (later numbered as 18-20). He was well known as the author of a number of school books: *Orthographical Exercises* (1793), a series of moral letters and a selection of essays from the best English writers, which ran to more than 20 editions, the last in 1863; *English Grammatical Exercises* (1795); and *Rudiments of Penmanship* (1797). This school was continued in the same premises from 1803 by Rev. Alexander Power, and from 1831 by John Underdown.

The 19th century saw a great increase in the number of private schools or academies. A directory of 1827 lists boarding schools (in addition to that of Power) for gentlemen run by Thomas Bourn, Thomas Hall, and Thomas Tappenden, and for ladies by Miss Burden and the Misses Rogers and Barker.

The Parliamentary report of 1837 states that £10 a year had been paid for 13 years from the charity founded by Thomas Turner (see below) to pay for the education of 10 poor boys in the academy of Thomas Power. (There is no other reference to 'Thomas Power', and this is likely to be a mistake for Alexander.) This had been discontinued in 1835 and a payment made to the national school instead. Mr. Power complained about this change, since he had paid £200 for the goodwill of the school, including £50 for the value of this annual payment.

Other schools were established lower down on the west side of Hempstead Street, in the buildings later numbered 50 and 52. These houses had been built by Arthur Apsley,

19 & 20. The old Grammar school in the churchyard, built in 1636. These two views show the large house to the north, used by the master and for boarders.

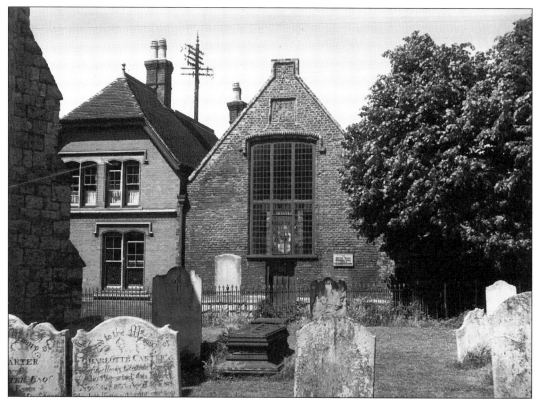

21.   *The old Grammar school, as the Dr. Wilks' Memorial Hall, pictured in 1972. The building now houses the Ashford museum.*

22.   *The school in the churchyard closed in 1870, and after a few years the foundation was transferred to a new school, shown here, in Hythe Road. These buildings are now part of the North school.*

a local builder and developer, about 1810, and they were used as a school for many years. The Misses Rogers and Barker occupied no. 52 from 1817, and Miss Charlotte Lester occupied no. 50. When they were sold in 1869 the premises were described as 'previously Alexander's academy, then St Augustine's college', and occupiers included Sarah Lester and Sarah and Martha Snoad in 1840, all described in directories as running schools. In 1869 the occupier was Mrs. Gertrude Ann Badham, who left in 1870 to open the 'collegiate' School at 10 High Street (now the *County Hotel*). The school in Hempstead Street continued from 1873 with Thomas Vie (previously head of the National school) as headmaster, who acquired both numbers 50 and 52.

The school started about 1816 by the National Society for the Education of the Poor in the Principles of the Established Church (usually referred to as the 'National' school) was housed in a building in Gravel Walk behind the workhouse, on land owned by the parish. This was replaced by the new school at Barrow Hill, which was built in 1841 to accommodate 440 pupils, also on land that belonged to the parish. The infants' school was enlarged in 1884. This school, now St Mary's primary school, continues to be used to educate some of the children of Ashford.

The population growth following the opening of the railway works led to demands for additional school provision, and in 1852 the Southern Railway Company were persuaded to provide the New Town school, originally with room for 550 children.

Both of these schools were sponsored by the established church, and non-conformist interests were met by the provision of a school on the Lancasterian principles. These schools were run by the British and Foreign School Society, founded in 1808 by Joseph Lancaster, a quaker, and were therefore usually called British schools.

Unfortunately the early records of the British school in Ashford were lost in the fire which destroyed Headley's printing works in 1906, but a programme printed for a bazaar held in November 1900 to raise funds for the school gives a short summary.

The opening of the school is said to be about 1840, and the first girls' teacher named as a Mrs. Tunbridge. Mrs. Ann Tunbridge is given as a schoolmistress in New Rents in the trade directory for 1838, so, unless this was a private school, the British school may have been in existence by this date. The school was started in New Rents, in premises later no. 12. This small building had been used as the Friends' Meeting House until 1802, and was probably still owned by a member of the Society of Friends. The 1900 programme says that Miss Letitia Hagger was the founder. She was a Quaker, and the aunt of Henry Headley, the grocer. The Headley family, and those related to them by marriage, were active workers for the British school throughout its existence.

Within a few years the school had outgrown the premises, and a new school was built in Forge Lane. This was a large school—a report in the *Kentish Express* for 17 May 1856 gives the number of pupils as 171 boys and 121 girls. Some twenty years later larger premises were again necessary, and the school moved to a new building in West Street, opening there on 10 February 1862 with accommodation for 480 pupils, and built at a cost of £1,465. It was enlarged in 1885 and 1904.

The old school was sold, and was converted to a public house, the *British Flag*. This building was demolished about twenty years ago for the ring road.

Developments in the education system, with the separation of junior and senior pupils, led to problems with the school, and it was finally agreed that the British school should be handed over to the County Council. This operated from the autumn of 1928, the new name being the Ashford West Street Council School, ending a period of nearly ninety years

23.   This building in Forge lane was erected about 1845 for the British school. It was sold to brewers in 1862, when the school moved to West street, and demolished when the ring road was constructed in the 1970s.

of voluntary effort. Within a few years all the pupils had been transferred to other Council schools, and the buildings were sold to the Salvation Army for use as their head-quarters. They have now gone, and the premises are today empty and derelict.

In 1870 Parliament passed the first Act which established schools run by a local authority as distinct from a voluntary body. School Boards were to be established where the schools provided were insufficient for the needs of the area. Such a board was started in Ashford in 1879 following an Act passed in 1876 that required for the first time that all children should receive educa-tion. The first Board school was that in Beaver Road, for 450 children. From 1880 attendance was compulsory until the age of 10 years, but up to 13 if the number of attendances had been below prescribed levels. Board (and later council) schools gradually spread, and replaced the voluntary schools for most of the children.

Charities were established for purposes other than education and, although they could have been described in the chapters dealing with their objectives, there are several reasons for dealing with them together here. Firstly, some of the objectives fall into two catego-ries—should a charity for the provision of education for the poor be regarded as a charity for education or one for the relief of the poor? Secondly, charities were controlled by the local gentry acting as trustees. The number of such persons in Ashford was quite limited, and the same individuals acted for several charities, and this led to confusion.

Then, the trustees were not as diligent as they should have been in appointing succes-sors to those who died. For Best's land no appointments were made after 1632. In 1842 application was made to the High Court for the position to be regularised. Before they would act the Court ordered an enquiry to ascertain whether any of those appointed in 1632 were still alive! Being satisfied with the evidence, they then named successors.

Lastly the administration was clarified in 1890 by the Charity Commissioners. Appli-cation for a scheme was made by the vicar, Rev. Peter Tindall, the churchwardens, George Wilks and Thomas Edwards, and Frederick Hughes-Hallett, Benjamin Kelly Thorpe, Edward Thurston, Robert Elliott, John Furley, John Russell Lewis, George Whitlock Greenhill and the Overseers of the Poor. The scheme was made by the Commissioners on 31 October, and provided for the following charities:

- for the maintenance of the Church: the charities of Sir John Fogge, [ ] Herbert, and John Asherst.
- for the further education of church of England scholars: the charity of Thomas Turner
- for the general benefit of the poor: the charities of Richard Best, Thomas Milles and Sir Richard Smith, Martha Copley, William Brett, and John Barlow.

The scheme established new rules for the appointment of trustees, who were to be:
- ex officio: the vicar and the churchwardens
- representative: four persons appointed for five years by the Local Board (later the Urban District Council)
- co-optative: elected by the other trustees for seven years.

Details of the property given to these charities to finance their objects are given in Appendix XI.

Towards the end of the 18th century a number of mutual help societies were formed. The earliest in Ashford was the Ashford Society for the Benefit of Widows, of which the first rules are dated 1795. This was followed in 1826 by the Ashford Benefit Society, first rules 1826, and the Ashford Benevolent Society in 1851. These societies were registered as Friendly Societies. In his will dated 1816, John Virrill left £25 to the 'Lying in Charity in Ashford'.

Branches of national Friendly Societies were also started in the town. Official reports of the Registrar of Friendly Societies give the Benefit Society of the St Stephen's Lodge of Oddfellows as starting in 1821, but an entry in the court rolls for 1840 gives 1806 as the date of establishment. By 1821 their funds were sufficient to advance £200 (with interest at five per cent) on mortgage to James Hamilton, a butcher in the High Street. Official returns give the Sir Edward Knatchbull Lodge of Oddfellows as dating from 1855, and lodges of the Ancient Order of Foresters from 1851 and 1852.

Almshouses to accommodate eight persons were built in 1853 on land given by George Elwick Jemmett in Tufton Street. They were financed by a legacy of £300 from James Wall, and public subscriptions of £340. Additional land was purchased at the rear with a legacy of £100 from Thomas Whitfeld. Various other bequests for the benefit of the occupants were made in the last century by Robert Furley and John Munns (postmaster for over 30 years), and further bequests later. In addition £312 17s. 0d. collected in the town to commemorate Queen Victoria's Diamond Jubilee was invested to provide an income for maintenance. These cottages were demolished to make way for the Tufton shopping centre (now County Square), and replaced by the bungalows in Vicarage Lane.

9

Highways, Canals and Railways

The increasing population, and the changing economic and social conditions of the Tudor period gave rise to the need for changes in the methods for the upkeep of the roads. The spread of commerce required improved forms of transport.

Until this period there had been no clearly defined responsibility for the upkeep of roads. More prosperous members of the community would leave money in their wills for the improvement of the road near their houses. Manor courts would attempt to see that ways were kept open, and that occupiers of the adjoining properties did not obstruct the road by depositing rubbish or erecting buildings.

The solution, introduced by an Act of Parliament in 1555, was similar in many respects to that adopted for the relief of the poor. The responsibility was placed on the parish, the inhabitants being required to elect annually one of their members as surveyor. This unpaid official had the responsibility of supervision, and could be required to account to the Justices if complaints were made as to the state of the highway. The work of maintenance was carried out by all householders, who were required to work for four days each year on the roads, under the directions of the surveyor. Those persons who occupied more extensive lands were required to provide carts with two men. An amending Act of 1563 increased the liability for 'statute labour' to six days a year, and this continued until 1835.

Despite these requirements, the state of the roads remained bad, especially if the subsoil was clay. Where the road crossed land that was of sand or gravel, which drained quickly, the situation was acceptable, but in areas such as the Weald, with deep clay, roads were often impassable for traffic during much of the winter, until the 19th century. Bridges were dealt with differently since rivers were commonly the boundary of parishes, and therefore maintenance was likely to be disputed by the two parishes. The responsibility for the major bridges was placed on the county, rather than the parish. Where this was not justified, the two adjoining parishes were required to share the work—a common source of argument.

In 1600 the inhabitants of the town of Ashford were before the Justices at Quarter Sessions at Canterbury, in a dispute with the inhabitants of the hundred of Chart (the administration of the rural area to the west of the town). The argument concerned the liability for repairs to the bridge at Beaver, on the road between Ashford and Romney Marsh. For Ashford it was argued by counsel that the inhabitants of the rural area hitherto shared in the cost of upkeep, a view contested by them. It was agreed that the decision should be made by the 'country' (county), and a jury of men from Felborough hundred (around Chilham) was chosen. Unfortunately the record of the final decision has not survived.

Another example concerned the road between Ashford and Challock, which was alleged in 1607 to be 'stopped'.

Over the succeeding centuries, many examples can be found of the deficiencies in both the system and in standard of maintenance that was achieved locally. There was continual resentment against the liability to statute labour. In 1651 Henry Downes of Ashford, yeoman, was before the Justices, charged with being 'in default of his wayne or cart for five whole days'. In the 18th century the inhabitants of Ashford were charged before the Justices with not repairing the road to Hythe in 1716, and to Maidstone in 1720. 1741 was a year for several complaints—the town for not repairing the road in North Lane, and four individuals for not repairing the pavement in front of their houses in the High Street.

The condition of Ashford bridge was clearly a considerable problem—complaints were made to the Justices in 1709, 1723, 1736, 1752, 1759, 1763, 1772, 1782, 1784, 1789, 1790 and 1795! This was despite a rebuilding that had taken place in 1683.

It had become apparent in many areas that the amount of work that could be carried out with statute labour was insufficient for the proper repair of the roads. To overcome this Parliament authorised in 1654 the levying of a 'cess' or rate on the inhabitants, to give the surveyor additional funds. At first temporary, the provision was made permanent in 1691. Application had to be made to the Justices, and this was done more commonly in Kent than in other counties. One disadvantage of being appointed parish surveyor was that the costs had to be met from the individual's own resources, hopefully to be repaid later. Thus in 1706 an application was made for a cess of 2d. on Ashford, 'whereas John Wightwick, Walter Rasell, Edward Vincer and Abraham Flint, late surveyors of Ashford have spent £13 4s. 9d. on highways'. This presumably means that monies had been spent by the various surveyors over four years, and only after the cess had been collected could they hope for reimbursement. Ten further levies were made in Ashford between 1706 and 1771, some for a cess of as much as 6d., and the 11 totalled 47d.

From time to time, these efforts were supplemented by the activities of individuals. In the period between 1780 and 1800 Henry Creed (in addition to his concern with the poor law administration) was active in getting the roads in the town centre paved. This work received the warm support of the Poor Law Commissioners in their report on Ashford in 1836, commenting that the work had been carried out at a cost less than that incurred elsewhere in the promotion of a local Act of Parliament. No doubt Creed sought the financial support of others for the work. In addition to paving, Creed bought several properties which stood in the centre of the High Street, east of Middle Row. These were demolished in order to widen the access.

Despite this work, the same legal procedure for the repair of the town roads continued until 1824. In that year the inhabitants of Ashford decided that the time had come for more effective action, and they promoted a local Act of Parliament for the appointment of Improvement Commissioners. A committee of local men was appointed with the responsibility for lighting, watching and paving the local roads. They continued to act until 1863 when a Local Board (the first local body elected by the inhabitants) took over, to be replaced in turn by the Urban District Council in 1894. Further details of the work of these bodies will be given in a later chapter.

The system outlined above had its difficulties in the maintenance of town roads. In country parishes, with much greater distances involved, the problems were much more serious. This was particularly the case where the parish had within its boundaries a road which was the main connection between major cities. In these cases the parishioners found themselves liable for the heavy costs of maintaining a road which was used mostly by outsiders, who made no contribution to the expense. The solution introduced by Parliament was the creation of turnpike roads—toll roads for which users had to pay.

The first such road was in 1663 for part of the Great North Road in Hertfordshire. The new system was slow to spread at first, and the first turnpike road in Kent was that between

Sevenoaks and Tunbridge Wells, authorised in 1709. In the following century the system was adopted widely, until by 1850 there were some 49 trusts in Kent, responsible for some 644 miles of highway, and collecting tolls at 291 gates. Apart from the improvement to the condition and widening of existing roads, turnpike trustees improved alignments and in some instances built completely new stretches. They created a new pattern of major roads that remained virtually undisturbed until the building of by-passes and motorways in this century.

For each turnpike, the procedure was that a group of local landowners would call a public meeting, at which financial and other support would be sought, and a committee appointed to promote a Bill. This would appoint a long list of local worthies as trustees, but in practice only a handful would take an active part in the administration of the trust. Since it was believed that, if sufficient money could be collected from tolls to put the highway in good order, this condition would then continue unaltered, the powers given by most Acts were limited to 21 years. It did not take long for it to become obvious that this was an extremely optimistic view, and it was necessary to obtain a continuance Act every 21 years.

As far as Ashford was concerned, there were four turnpikes responsible for the roads leading out of the town. Taking them in the order in which they were created, they were:

1762—for the road from Faversham to Ashford and then to Hythe, and for the branch that led from Ashford to Canterbury. These roads had a total mileage of 36½, the second longest of any trust in the county, but had only seven gates at which tolls were collected.

1767—for the road from Ashford to Bethersden, Biddenden and Tenterden, totalling 18½ miles, controlled by 18 gates.

1793—for the road from Ashford to Maidstone, also 18½ miles, with 10 gates.

1793—for the road from Ashford to just beyond Hamstreet. This was only eight and a half miles, with eight gates.

It will be seen that, despite the difficulties of the steep hill from Boughton Aluph to Challock, the road that was regarded as the most important, and therefore turnpiked first, was that from Faversham. This was because, until the coming of the railways, it was more convenient and economic for heavy goods to be transported by water as near as possible to their destination. At the end of the 18th century the parish was buying coal for the workhouse from a merchant in Faversham, and there is no doubt that this was the traditional route for most heavy goods coming to Ashford. The same route was used for journeys to London, the road through Maidstone which we regard as obvious today being of little importance until the early 19th century. The improvements made by the turnpike and the introduction of stage coaches on this route brought a complete change.

The day-to-day management of the roads was in the hands of officers, a clerk (often a local solicitor) and, most importantly, a surveyor. In Ashford the surveyor of the turnpikes from 1820 was Thomas Thurston, who in addition was employed over a wide area for roads and later railways. There were many problems with the roads, and attempts were made in continuance Acts to overcome them. On the one hand local inhabitants objected to paying tolls for short and frequent journeys, and exemptions were given to persons going to church, and for agricultural work.

The turnpike trustees were anxious to limit damage to their roads, and schedules of charges were amended to increase the payment due from heavy carts that had wheels with

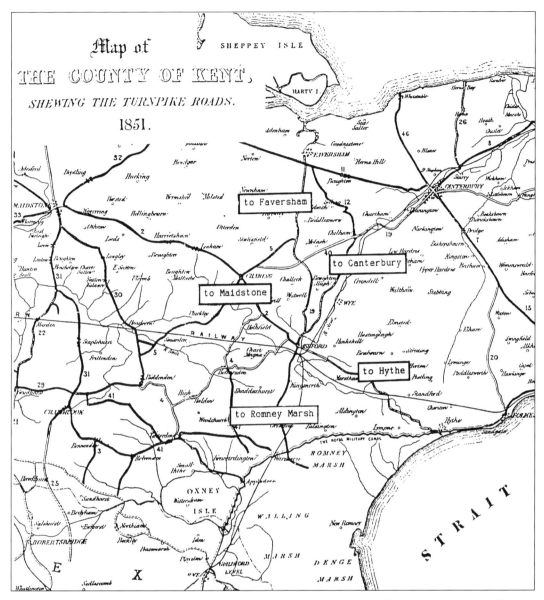

24.   *Map of the turnpike roads in 1851, showing the five routes leading from Ashford. The map also shows four railways—the fifth, to Maidstone, was not opened until 1884.*

narrow rims. Some idea of the regulations made can be seen in the poster illustrated on page 52.

In addition, the turnpike trustees had problems in the collection of tolls. They often avoided this by letting them for a period of a year to a contractor, who paid a lump sum and hoped to make a profit on the working. One of the problems was with the collectors—in 1836 information was laid by Frederick Underdown of Ashford that the collector at the Willesborough gate had not issued a ticket for the toll of 3d. that had been paid by Henry Vile.

TURNPIKE ROADS.

From Ashford to Maidstone.
From Ashford to Tenterden.
From Maidstone to Biddenden.
From Ashford to Hamstreet.
From Biddenden to Bound Gate,
From Charing to Chilham,

From Ashford to { Canterbury, Faversham, and Hythe,

From Appledore (thro Tenterden) to Cranbrook,
From Castleton's Oak (thro Biddenden) to Milkhouse Street.

And the Woodchurch Turnpike Roads.

The Trustees of the above Roads have resolved to enforce the following provisions of the General Turnpike Acts.

Persons Driving without Reins

and riding on any Waggon or Cart upon any Turnpike Road, without some other Person on foot or on horseback to guide the horse or horses therein, and such horses not being more than two drawing the same; are liable to a penalty of FORTY SHILLINGS.   3 Geo. 4, cap. 126. sec. 132.

Owner's Name of every Waggon

Wain, Cart, or other such Carriage, shall be painted in one or more straight lines upon some conspicuous part of the right or off side, or upon the off side shafts thereof; if such name or place of abode be false or fictitious, or if such Carriage be used on any Turnpike Road without such name &c, the owner is liable to a penalty of FIVE POUNDS.   Sec. 15.

Any Driver leaving Block Stones

on any Turnpike Road after having blocked or stopped any Cart, Waggon, or other Carriage in going up a hill, is liable to a penalty of FORTY SHILLINGS, over and above the damage caused thereby; and descending a hill with a wheel locked without a skidpan, to a penalty of TWENTY SHILLINGS.   Sec. 121, and 124.

Any Hawker, Higgler, Gipsy,

or other person who shall pitch any Tent or encamp on any Turnpike Road or shall LEAVE ANY WAGGON, CART, or other Carriage upon the side thereof, longer than is necessary to load or unload the same, (except in case of accident, and then no longer than may be necessary to remove the same,) or IF ANY PERSON SHALL LAY ANY TIMBER, MANURE, or other thing whatsoever upon, or on the sides thereof, he shall be liable to a penalty of FORTY SHILLINGS.   Sec. 124.

If any Horse, Sheep, Beast,

or Cattle of any kind, be found tethered, wandering, straying, or lying about any Turnpike Road, the same will be impounded, and a penalty of TWO SHILLINGS per head will be enforced. 4, Geo. 4, c. 96, Sec. 78.

By Order of the Trustees,

THOMAS THURSTON,

ASHFORD, August 26, 1847.   SURVEYOR.

Elliott and Son, Printers, Ashford.

25.   A notice issued by Thomas Thurston as surveyor to several Turnpike Trusts in 1847. It shows that the Trustees had far wider powers than the upkeep of the road.

Whatever their difficulties and drawbacks, there can be no doubt that the turnpikes transformed the road transport system. They enabled a much improved network of stage coaches to operate throughout the country. In Kent there were by 1830 regular services including those from Ashford to Maidstone and London, to Canterbury and to Hythe, as well as connections to the smaller towns. The turnpikes were also of great significance in the establishment of postal services on a regular basis. Financially, however, they had difficulties, which became a crisis in many cases as railways began to spread after 1840. Some trusts were never in a strong financial position—enthusiasm had led to roads being turnpiked for which the volume of traffic was too small, and the tolls were not even sufficient to pay the interest on loans borrowed to carry out the work on the roads. For these trusts the future was bleak, each year leaving them deeper in debt.

The first railway to affect the Ashford area was the line opened from Canterbury to Whitstable in 1830, followed by the opening of new harbour facilities in 1836. This route provided a new method of travel to London on a route not greatly different from that of the old roads before the Maidstone road was turnpiked. Coaches were run from the *George* in Ashford to connect with the trains, and then by steamer from Whitstable. The service was available only three times a week in each direction, so the numbers using it could only have been small.

The South Eastern Railway from London reached Ashford at the end of 1842. The immediate effect on the turnpike traffic was mixed. Where the road ran more or less parallel with the railway, the fall in receipts from tolls was large and immediate. Where the railway ran across the road network, the reverse might apply, since more traffic would be generated on the roads by those going to the railway stations.

For the four Ashford trusts the position can be judged from the following table:

	Toll income for the year		
	1834	1841	1849
	£	£	£
Ashford to Faversham etc.	1,855	1,772	1,373
Ashford to Bethersden etc.	806	758	661
Ashford to Maidstone	1,515	1,886	1,030
Ashford to Hamstreet	399	333	405

It will be seen that (with the exception of the road to Maidstone) receipts were declining before then. Tolls on the road from the Marsh increased after the railway reached Ashford in 1842, with more people coming from that area to join the train.

Nationally, the position of many turnpike trusts was desperate by 1850, and Parliament called for general reports. That for Kent (the first) was published in 1851, giving much detailed information on all the trusts in the county. One table shows the number of year's tolls that would be necessary to repay the debt. For one trust in mid-Kent, this was 294 years! The Ashford trusts were in better shape, the least happy being the road to Hamstreet, which despite the increased receipts would have required seven years' tolls to repay the debt.

As a result of these enquiries, turnpike trusts were gradually abolished. The responsibility for the main roads was transferred to Highways Boards, set up for areas in many cases the same as the poor law unions. In 1889 the responsibility was given to the newly formed County Councils. Details of the local Acts applying to the trusts in the Ashford area, and of their finances, will be found in Appendix XII.

As was mentioned earlier, transport on water was always preferred if at all possible. This is the one geographical feature which Ashford lacks. The river Stour is not large enough for boats of any size, the port nearest to the town for goods from London or the north being Faversham. It is a matter for conjecture as to whether the town would have expanded to a far greater extent had the Stour been a much bigger river.

26. *Nearly all of the houses built in the last century south of the railway were for employees in the railway work. The railway company contributed to the cost of amenities, including shops, baths and this church.*

During the late 18th and early 19th centuries many canals were built in England, and proposals were made for a canal joining the north east of Kent with the Weald. An Act authorising the works was passed by Parliament in 1812, but the scheme failed to get the necessary backing, and the canal was never built.

The railway was to have a far greater effect on the town. The scheme was widely supported by tradesmen, who gave evidence before the Parliamentary committee in 1836 as to the benefits that they expected. Thus Samuel Steddy, describing himself as a timber merchant who had lived in Ashford for 53 years, said he was unable to meet the demand for timber from the London market because of the difficulties of transport in the winter when the roads were in a very bad condition. Similar views were expressed by George Hayward, butcher, William Jefferies, grocer, and John Dungey, ironmonger. William Walter, landlord (of the *Saracen's Head*) complained of the cost of transporting spirits and porter, as well as coal, all brought from Faversham in his own wagons.

The line from London (via Redhill) was built by the South Eastern Railway Company, which opened the Ashford station on 1 December 1842. By 1850 the lines to Folkestone, Canterbury, and to Hastings were all in use. The working life of the town was transformed by the decision of the railway company to site their main works at Ashford, resulting in the building of Newtown and a great increase in the population. The railway from Maidstone was not opened until 1884, being built by the great rivals of the South Eastern Company, the London and Chatham Railway. Originally there was no connection with the lines of the South Eastern, their station being off Godinton Road, where the railway goods yard is now.

By the end of the 19th century Ashford had become a 'railway town', as important to the South Eastern as Swindon to the Great Western. They were the largest employers, and the largest ratepayers. They contributed to the establishment of the church in South Ashford, and to the school at Newtown. They expected to be consulted by the local authority on new proposals for the town, but there were occasions when the two had differences. Thus, in August 1872 the Local Board addressed a 'Humble Petition' to the Company, supporting a parishioner who complained of the inadequacy of third-class accommodation, and the late arrival of goods trains. In reply the Company cited their expenditure on schools, the church and the high cost of coal as reasons why they could make no improvement.

Further details of the development and impact of the railway on Ashford here can be found the book by Gordon Turner, first published in 1984, *Ashford—The Coming of the Railway*.

10

Crime and Punishment

A number of studies in recent years have shown that, until the 18th century, violence was common in everyday life. One writer says '... in the rural villages of seventeenth century England violence was always just below the surface, and frequently erupted ... the average peasant was a short-tempered, malicious character who flared into physical violence on the flimsiest excuse'. Another writer describes the situation: 'stealing and robbery were endemic ... murder and manslaughter were frequent'. The reason for this widespread brutality is stated as 'life in a world where pestilence and famine were regular, was indeed very cheap'.

In general the position was at its worst in the more isolated parts of the country, particularly the north. However, where there were physical features of the countryside that made escape from the forces of law and order easier, violence persisted. Ashford was not itself in an isolated position, but was on the fringe of two such areas.

Firstly, the great forest of the Weald. This was a relatively isolated place until the improvement of the roads in the late 18th century, and the coming of the railway in the 19th. It had been for centuries a place of escape for rebels of all sorts. It was in particular the place of refuge for the religious non-conformists of the 16th and 17th centuries.

The other influence was the proximity of the coast, and the opportunity for smuggling. Throughout the 18th and early 19th centuries, a state of continual fighting existed between the various gangs of smugglers and the excise men and soldiers sent to prevent their trade. Again, Ashford was not the centre of this activity, but close enough for the events to be well known, and to influence the attitudes of many of the townspeople. In 1749 a proclamation issued by the secretary to the Customs House in London listed the names of a large number of persons wanted in connection with an assembly for smuggling, including James Brooksey, a patten maker of Ashford.

Perhaps the most surprising evidence of dual standards in this question was Dr. Isaac Rutton, a well known Ashford citizen, a Justice of the Peace, a substantial landowner and a regular attender at social events at Mersham with the Knatchbull family. He was the son of Matthias Rutton of Ashford and Sarah, daughter of Nicholas Toke of Godinton. Yet recent research has shown that Rutton was the leader of the 'Seasalter Company', a group of men engaged in smuggling on a large scale. Goods were landed on the north-Kent coast, and carried overland to Lenham and thence to London. Two of Rutton's sons were also probably involved—Isaac, the eldest, who lived for a time at Ospringe, and Matthias, who was vicar of Sheldwich and rector of Badlesmere and Leaveland. All of these places are conveniently placed on the route to Lenham.

In 1808 Messrs. Jemmett & Son, solicitors, were paid (somewhat late!) for prosecuting the notorious smugglers, James and William Ransley at the Spring Assizes, 1800. From these events, and others detailed later, it is clear that the inhabitants of Ashford must have been well aware of violent events in the area. Further evidence is provided by the post. Mail coaches, equipped with an iron safe for the letters and carrying an armed guard, had first been introduced from London to Bath in 1784. By the autumn of 1785 they had entirely replaced the old system of post-boys on horseback on the routes between all the major towns. On the subsidiary routes post-boys continued and, in 1831, when post for Ashford from London came via Canterbury, they were armed.

By the middle of the 19th century prize-fighting with bare fists was illegal, but continued despite this. On 5 April 1859 Tom Sayers, the British champion, fought Bill Benjamin near Headcorn. A special train was run from London, and hundreds of people, described in the *Kentish Express* as 'London roughs', attended. Police were sent from Ashford to break up the gathering, which they did after two fights had taken place. The Hone Office raised the matter with the directors of the railway company, but they claimed not to have known of the arrangements for the train, 'which were made by their servants'. They promised not to allow a repeat.

The Tudor period had seen a great increase in the number of vagrants, bands of wandering beggars who created great terror in country districts. The underlying reason for the increase of such persons was unemployment, due to changing social conditions and the numbers of discharged soldiers. On the other hand, a large number of persons of higher social class can be found amongst those before the courts charged with violent crimes.

Parliament passed legislation designed to cope with the situation. As with poor relief and highway administration, this involved the parish officers. The most important was the very ancient office of constable. These had been appointed by the Court Leet of a manor from Norman times, and had specific duties under the Statute of Winchester of 1285 for supervising the local arrangements for public safety. In addition to the parish constable (often called 'petty constable', or, in Kent, 'borsholder'), a constable was appointed for the hundred, an administrative division of the county originating in Saxon times.

The constable was the last link in a chain. They were supervised by the local Justices of the Peace, who were appointed by the Crown on the advice of the Lord Lieutenant of the county from 1360. The Justices, in addition to deciding some matters themselves, met each quarter in Quarter Sessions—in Kent at Canterbury for East Kent, and Maidstone for the western part of the county. The most serious of crimes were referred to the King's justices, who toured the country holding trials at the Assizes.

The records of Quarter Sessions have survived for East Kent from the 16th century, and we can read accounts of some of the crimes committed by the people of Ashford. In many respects they are very similar to those of today. Thus the Assizes in 1559 dealt with the case of the death of James Grene. A number of men, including servants of Sir John Fogge, were in a field called 'Moyse Pitts' at Ashford. A fight broke out, during which Grene was killed by a blow from a hazel staff by Richard Kingsnorth. His plea of self defence was accepted by the jury, and Kingsnorth was pardoned. In 1563 the same Court found James Purser of Ashford not guilty of the rape of Agnes Wevell, aged 12 years.

An indication of the general violent conditions can be seen from a case of 1604. William Cox had been arrested by the constable, Thomas March, charged with stabbing George Holt, a tailor. Cox escaped but Hugh Tritton, the borsholder (the petty constable) tried to re-arrest him at a house in Kennington. He was prevented from this by John Cox senior (the keeper of the *Saracen's Head*, and presumably the father of William) and his wife Anna, John Cox junior (a brother), and Benedict and Thomas Cox, who 'riotously assembled and threatened Hugh Tritton'.

Quarter Sessions cases were more likely to be concerned with theft, sometimes of cash but more often of sheep or other farm animals. In January 1598 Thomas Wilson of Ashford, saddler, was indicted for the assault of Mary, wife of Robert Allen, and the theft of a purse containing five shillings in cash and a gold ring. Because of the amount involved, the case was sent to the Assizes. The decision is unknown. In 1656 a coroner's inquest was held on Henry Lethbetter, the keeper of the *Saracen's Head*. Evidence was given that 'James Bowling, joiner, was moved by the instigation of the Divell to throw an iron file at Lethbetter', hitting him on the head and causing his death three weeks later.

Quarter Sessions also dealt with trading cases. In 1614 John Harker of Ashford was charged with 'exercising the trade of miller, and not having been apprenticed'. Three months later Harker was making the same charge against Peter Cole of Ashford. At the same time Peter Cole was alleging that Edward Ellis of Great Chart was engrossing grain, that is, attempting to buy the whole or a substantial part of the supply, in order to sell it at higher prices. Obviously there was considerable rivalry and animosity between the millers at this time.

During the Commonwealth period there was a national increase in cases of alleged witchcraft, and there was one case in Ashford. The accused was Wilman, the wife of George Worsiter, a sawyer of Ashford. The person bewitched was a girl of 13 years, Sarah the daughter of John Harris, a shoemaker. Several residents gave evidence that they had seen the girl ill and having strange fits. The suggestion that she was bewitched was apparently made by Anthony Harlott, a mariner from the 'Isle of Garnesey'. In the end, Worsiter was found not guilty. Harlott appears to have been a determined 'witch-hunter'—a month later he was making similar allegations about a woman of Boughton Aluph.

27.   *The* Saracen's Head, *at one time the most important inn or hotel in the town. In 1656 its keeper was the victim of murder.*

A case demonstrating the concerns of the period is recorded in 1666. Two Ashford men gave evidence that they had met William Barrett, a gunsmith of Ashford, who had asked 'what news?'. On being told that it was said that 8,000 Dutch had invaded, Barrett was alleged to have replied, 'they were fools if they did not do as much mischief to our nation as we had done to theirs'. The decision in this case of sedition is unknown.

Cases of theft, assault and the occasional more serious crime continued. From the early part of the 18th century most cases were dealt with by the Justices, either singly or in pairs, and increasingly in Petty Sessions. These meetings of the Justices for an area began informally, but by the middle of the 17th century formal meetings on a regular timetable were being held. Very few records of these early meetings have been found, but the minute book for the Ashford division (responsible for the area around Ashford and much of Romney Marsh) for the period 1773-93 has survived. Seventeen Justices acted during those years, only two of whom lived in the town—Robert Mascall and Dr. Isaac Rutton (the smuggler). The vast majority of cases concerned poor relief, but other cases including assault and one of desertion from the army were also decided.

One of the difficulties with law enforcement was the lack of both the personnel and the finance to pursue and prosecute alleged criminals. An example of this can be seen in 1783, when the Ashford Vestry voted up to £5 5s. 0d. to support the prosecution of John Huntley, committed on a charge of the murder of a woman 'supposed his wife' on Westwell Downs.

From the earliest times, it was necessary to have some form of prison where those charged could be held. The lord of the manor had a 'cage', a cellar, underneath the original market hall in Middle Row—it is still there. Later he had a lock-up behind the buildings at the top of the High Street that later became no. 109. At the end of the 18th century, the parish had a lock-up on their land behind the workhouse in Forge Lane. It was not until the early 19th century that any form of professional police were appointed. The local Act of Parliament in 1824 was sought because 'of frequent depredations and theft in the night time'. Three watchmen were appointed at a wage of 12s. a week. The status of the watchmen may be judged by an incident in 1839, when one of them, Thomas Brooker, was dismissed for assaulting another watchman. Twelve months later he was re-appointed, there being no other applicant for the post! The following year the first policemen were appointed, under the superintendence of Walter Smith, until then with the Canterbury force. One of the conditions of service of the police was that 'they were not to leave the Town on any pretence without finding and paying a substitute'. Smith was not a success. In July 1842 he resigned after being charged with being drunk and having a loaded pistol whilst on duty.

With the establishment of the County Force in 1857, the local police were dismissed, and Ashford had a detachment under the control of a superintendent. This did not mean the end of difficulties. In 1870 the superintendent, George English, stole money from a prisoner and then went off to Australia with a lady friend. From a number of clues the police concluded that he would arrive in due course at Brisbane. They sent a constable in pursuit, and he, travelling by the 'overland route' (via Suez), arrived in Australia long before English, whose ship sailed round the Cape of Good Hope. English was arrested and brought back to receive a sentence of seven years' imprisonment.

The County Council are the police authority today, with headquarters in Ashford for a division responsible for a large area of south-east Kent.

11

The 18th Century

———————————

By the middle of the 18th century, Ashford was established as the market centre of the area. The political and religious controversies of the previous centuries were of less significance, and the townspeople could concentrate on their everyday life. We have seen how, during this period, many improvements had been made, such as the paving of the streets, and the beginnings of a representative local governing body.

The street scene had changed from that in medieval times. The timber-framed houses had, for the most part, either been demolished or, in many cases, altered to the outward appearance of the fashion of the period. The built-up area had grown, the town extending from the top of New Rents to the bottom of East Hill, and from North Street (from about where the ring road now runs) to the south side of the churchyard. New Street was still largely undeveloped with a farm on the north side and Barrow Hill a hamlet separate from the town. The population by 1750 was probably about 1,550, and grew quite rapidly to 2,000 by the end of the century.

In these more prosperous times, social gatherings were common. Although not on the scale of the events in the county capitals of Canterbury and Maidstone, Ashford was the recognised centre for the surrounding area. The *Saracen's Head* was the venue in the 18th century, and Canterbury newspapers carried advertisements, as for example, in December 1751: 'assemblies for dancing and cards on Monday 30 December, and then monthly every Thursday after the full moon'. These are reported in the diaries of some of those who attended, including Mrs. Elizabeth Montagu (the celebrated blue-stocking) and, in the early years of the next century, Jane Austen. She visited Ashford on a number of occasions whilst staying with her brother Edward Knight who lived at Godmersham.

Assemblies reached their peak during the Napoleonic wars, when thousands of troops were stationed in and around Ashford. This led to a demand for better facilities, and a lease was taken of the old court house (in Middle Row, now King's Parade) and a 'suite of public rooms for assemblies for amusement and recreation of dancing and cards' was erected. To defray the cost £1,025 was subscribed, the largest contribution being £75 from Lewis Whitfeld, a partner of the Ashford Bank, living in North Street. Sir Edward Knatchbull of Mersham Hatch gave £50, the balance coming from 36 subscribers of £25 each. In 1840 it was reported that the assemblies had been discontinued, and new subscribers were found to purchase the rights to the lease. This continued until 1892, the premises being used for various public and commercial purposes. In that year the lease was sold to the Local Board.

Action had been taken in 1671 by the lord of the manor, Viscount Strangford to confirm the legal authority for the market. The details are given in Appendix VI. This market continued in the lower High Street, on alternate Tuesdays. There is a well known print of this scene in the early part of the 19th century.

The wills of the period show clearly that all the trades necessary for daily life were represented in the town, as well as those providing essential support to the agriculture of the surrounding district. The wills also indicate the increasing prosperity of many of the inhabitants.

One of the trades essential to a market town, where large numbers of persons congregate on market days, is that of places providing food, drink and accommodation. The establishment of drinking houses in this country goes back many centuries, and by the 15th century there were three different classes. Alehouses, were the simplest and consisted solely of a room, part of an ordinary dwelling, where ale and, from the 16th century, beer (that is ale brewed with the addition of hops) could be purchased and drunk. Inns were the equivalent of the smaller hotel today, the important difference being that overnight accommodation could, and in later years had to, be provided. Taverns, strictly speaking, were for the sale of wine only. These were thought to be the highest class. Of course, in practice the distinctions were seldom as clearcut as they appear on paper. Spirits were introduced in the early Tudor period, but did not become common until the middle of the 18th century.

Officialdom was always interested in the control of those providing drink, if only to safeguard the quality of what was sold. Parishes appointed an aletaster to make the rounds, and to ensure the fitness of the drink. Although unpaid, it would seem likely that this post was accepted more readily than other parish offices, such as that of constable or overseer of the poor. In the time of Henry VIII it was thought that drinking, and the number of alehouses, was increasing alarmingly, and greater control was introduced by making it necessary to obtain a licence from the Justices. The reasons for exercising control were not to restrict drinking, but the wish to stop drinking on Sundays during the time of church services (attendance was compulsory) and the use of alehouses as places for seditious plotting. Victuallers were required to give security of £10 and to find two other persons to find two other sureties in £5 each. The undertaking they had to sign was as follows:

> A B acknowledges debt to the King of £10, and C D & E F of £5 each as sureties on condition that A B is admitted and allowed by the Justices to keep a common Alehouse or tippling house of A B, known by the sign of X, and not elsewhere, in the parish of Y if A B during such time as he shall keep the common alehouse shall not permit or suffer any unlawful Play or Game to be used in his said dwelling house or in his garden or orchard, especially by Men Servants, Apprentices, Common Labourers or idle Persons, but do and shall maintain, use and keep good Order and Rule.

Examples of the enforcement of these laws in Ashford include: in 1601 John Walton imprisoned for unlicensed victualling, Robert Jego summonsed for the same offence in 1615, and Nicholas Parris in 1630. Another example is the report in 1606 that 'Abraham Fusse suffered Edward Maynes and George Hayward to play at tables in his house in the time of divine service'. This was still causing problems in 1785, when it was alleged that several persons were drinking in the *George*, *White Hart*, and *Castle* alehouses during the time of divine service.

The only great relaxation in the control of the sale of beer was brought about by the Beerhouse Act of 1830. This allowed anyone to be given a licence to sell beer, without having to give sureties to the Justices. But criticism followed very quickly. By 1834 justices in Ashford were saying that 'no single measure ever caused so much mischief in so short a time, by demoralising the labourers'. The constable of Ashford said that 'all the fires that were a feature of the agricultural riots in those years were perpetrated by frequenters of beershops'. The control of beershops by the Justices was re-introduced in 1869.

When considering the actual premises in Ashford the pride of place today must be given to the *George*, which is the only substantial inn that still exists in premises that go back at least to the 16th century. The first reference that we know is in a will of 1533. It seems likely that it declined in importance in the 18th century, when (as mentioned earlier) it was described as an alehouse. Although the name must refer to St George, since it was called the *George* long before we had a king of that name, there is no documentary evidence to support the suggestion that it was once called 'George and Dragon'.

The major inn in the town for many centuries was the *Saracen's Head*. It may have existed as early as the 14th century, and almost certainly developed out of the lodgings provided for the stewards of the Manor. From 1382 the lords of the manor were the Dean and Chapter of the Chapel of St Stephen in Westminster. As absentee landlords they would send a steward to visit the area every six months or so, to collect the rents and to settle disputes in the Lord's Court. Accommodation would be provided and there are examples elsewhere of those premises being made available to others when not required

28. *A picture of the* George *hotel at the beginning of this century. This is the only surviving inn still carrying on business in premises built in the 16th century.*

by the stewards. The site remained in the personal possession (but not occupation) of the lord of the manor until about 1805. This timber-framed building did not have the return frontage to North Street, but only a narrower frontage to the High Street, and was demolished in about 1860. The building that replaced it will be remembered by many, and was demolished in 1980.

Some details of the various premises that have been used as inns or alehouses over the centuries are given in Appendix XIV.

12

Military Matters

It will be obvious from what has been said of the advantages of Ashford as a centre of the surrounding area, that it is the natural place in which to base troops. It is not surprising, therefore, to find references to their presence throughout the centuries.

In 1569 the government was anxious to encourage an increase in the numbers skilled in the use of the harquebus, an early form of gun. A commission of enquiry was established, and they reported from Ashford on the available resources of men and weapons, and on the cost of establishing practice places and giving rewards to those who were trained.

From early Tudor times, all able-bodied men were liable to serve in the Militia, a body that could be called out in an emergency to help defend the country. They were not liable for overseas service, but by relieving the regular army made more men available for that purpose. The county militia was nominally under the command of the Lord Lieutenant, but in practice this responsibility was delegated to deputy lieutenants. A general muster (an inspection of the force) was made from time to time. The parish constable was responsible for recruiting the required number of men from his parish.

Attendance at muster clearly raised objections from some people, either from specific opposition to the purpose of the militia, or merely to the interruption to daily life. In 1635 four Ashford men were sent for by warrant, to explain their absence from a muster on 27 May in that year. They were excused on promising not to default again.

The growing opposition to the policies of Charles I in financial matters has already been referred to in chapter 5. Charles also aroused great fears in religious matters, particularly in Scotland. Many people in England thought that he wished to introduce Arminian (anti-Calvinistic) principles, supplanting the doctrines of the established church and the Act of Uniformity. The controversy was even stronger in Scotland, where Charles wished to restore an espiscopal instead of the presbyterian form of the Scottish church. By 1640 this led to armed intervention. Although the troops sent to Scotland were mainly from the north of England, the militia were called out throughout England in order to have replacements for those men sent over the border. The strength of the objection in Kent can be judged from the following letter written from Ashford by the deputy lieutenant (in command of the militia) to Philip, Earl of Pembroke and Lord Lieutenant of Kent on 11 May 1640:

> This day service has made such several advances and retreats, that we are bold to represent them to you. A wary and cheerful 'manage' on the part of Sir Humphrey Tufton was upon the soldiers until the latter part of the day when an unlooked for silence, followed by a stubborn sullenness, possessed the rest of the soldiers and infected the former to the defeat of our better expectations. In short we find a confusion. Some will not go beyond their colours, others will not go into Scotland, all are yeomen and farmers who say they must be as assuredly undone by going as refusing, so the list cannot yet be made up. They all hope to be relieved by impressed men, if they can be found, which if you will yield unto us as a present remedy of a distempered cause, will give good settlement to the many. They

have thrust out their rugged resolutions in this language 'take one and take all' and then forsaking rank and file they fell into disorder not to be reduced by the command of their officers.

These actions are obviously close to mutiny, and give an insight to the feelings of many just before the outbreak of the civil war.

Another illustration of the position of Ashford as a centre for troops is shown in a comment by the Earl of Thanet in the latter part of the 17th century. He wrote:

Sandhurst farm, with the Repton lands was emparked [fenced and used for deer] by the Earl's father about 1640 ... it was a park of at least seven miles in circumference, but it lay so far from Hothfield [the main residence of the Earl], and so near to the town of Ashford, where in the late rebellious times soldiers were always quartered who could not be kept from killing the deer ... it was disparked and turned at again into a farm.

The possibility of a Dutch landing during the 1650s was of great concern. In 1652 a troop of horse was stationed at Ashford, but was ordered to Deal in order to be immediately available if a landing were attempted. Troops were in Ashford in the following decades— Prince Rupert's Dragoons in 1678, as well as a foot regiment.

By the end of the century, the usual reason for troops in the area was to combat smuggling. As well as the bringing of goods into the country from abroad, this also involved traffic in the other direction. During this period the export of wool was prohibited. English wool had a very high reputation for quality, and was much sought after by continental weavers. The ban on the export of wool was intended to reduce the risk of unemployment of weavers in this country by increasing the export of finished cloth. Dragoons were stationed in Ashford from 1698 for a number of years.

In the middle of the 18th century, Scottish troops were stationed in the town. They must have been established for some time, and have had their wives and families with them. Being members of the presbyterian Church of Scotland, they attended the Independent (Congregational) Church in Ashford, and the church register records the baptism of their children.

Conflict between the King and Parliament over the control of the army had been an important factor leading to the outbreak of the Civil War, and in the overthrow of James II in 1688. When Parliament 'appointed' William of Orange and Mary as sovereigns they made sure that they kept ultimate control. One consequence was that there were no permanent quarters for troops, and an important function of inns in the 18th century was to provide accommodation for soldiers. From the records of payments in 1755 we know that dragoons of the Scot's Greys were billeted in Ashford, and can judge the relative size of the inns. Landlords were paid 1s. 7d. per week for: *Saracen's Head*, 23 men; *Lyon*, 9; *Crown*, 17; *White Hart*, 6; *Royal Oak*, 16; *Castle*, 5; *George*, 14; *Marlborough*, 4; *Bull*, 9. It is not surprising that landlords were far from happy with this requirement, although the rates of pay on that occasion were much lower than usual. In 1735 they complained to the Justices that grocers were selling strong liquor to the soldiers, and they too ought to have troops billeted on them. The grocers' excuse was that they did not know that this was taking place, as they had not been at home. This excuse was accepted by the Justices!

Until the end of the 18th century the number of troops stationed in Ashford at any one time was quite small. This was to change dramatically with the war against Napoleon. Ashford would have been (as again in the 1939-45 war) in the front line had an invasion occurred and the enemy obtained a foothold. A defensive line was proposed by General Sir David Dundas in 1796, running from Sussex through Ashford to Thanet. In order to feed the large number of men that might be sent into a locality, strategic magazines of biscuit for the men and forage for the horses were established, 'since in the first moment of hurry, it could not be expected that Ovens should be set going, and deliveries of bread made'. This magazine (which has given its name to the road) was at the junction with Canterbury Road, about where the new road to Maidstone is now. The site was sold by the War Office in 1821.

In addition, barracks were constructed at Barrow Hill, on the site of the present school. These must have been of a temporary nature—the contemporary equivalent of 'nissen huts', and were demolished after the war. There is no truth in the statement that the houses in Barrow Hill Row etc. were constructed as married quarters for the troops at this time—they were built about the middle of the last century.

The barracks were very extensive, and in the peak years, around 1800, held over 2,000 men; more, in fact, than the civilian population at the time of the first census of 1801. In addition to accommodation for the troops, there was a parade ground, stabling and a military hospital.

Most of the troops were militia of various counties, whose duties included helping with the construction of new roads. For two years from 1798 they constructed a new stretch of road to straighten the turnpike road between Chart Leacon and Great Chart. Although no record has been found, it is also likely that they carried out similar work on the road to Maidstone between the present junction with Warren Lane and the entrance to the Warren.

Regular troops were also billeted in the area before being sent abroad. Journals or memoirs have been published of members of the 43rd Light Infantry and the 71st Highland (Foot) Regiment, in which they describe a period spent in Ashford. It was during this period that Ashford had a member of the royal family living in the town. A property deed of 1798 states that the house in the High Street (on the site where Lloyds Bank now stands) was occupied by 'Lieutenant General, His Royal Highness William, Duke of Gloucester'. Although he is described in this way, William was not in fact entitled to be 'Royal Highness', since he was only the great-grandson of a sovereign (George II). Only when he married Mary, daughter of King George III in 1816 did he become entitled to the description. A year later he had gone, but the house was then used by officers of the Queen's Regiment, the 2nd Regiment of Foot.

By an Act of Parliament passed in 1795, Kent was required to provide 440 men for the Navy. The number required was apportioned to each parish on the basis of the number of inhabited houses. For Ashford this resulted in four men being required. A bounty, to be raised from the parish rates, was paid to each man, who did not have to live in the parish. Ashford found one 'volunteer' from Hythe, aged 19, and paid him £12 12s. 0d. One from Lympne and one from Whitstable were paid £21 each, whilst the last from Egerton received £18 18s. 0d. The procedure was repeated in 1796, when Ashford had to find five men, and in 1797 another four. Parishes failing to provide their full quota were fined.

After the defeat of Napoleon, a long period of peace in Europe meant an end to the stationing of troops in Ashford. Not until 1859 did a threat from Napoleon III result in the formation of the East Kent Volunteers—the equivalent of the Territorial Army. An Ashford (H) Company was formed in 1860, when 60 persons enrolled. A full history of the Volunteers can be found in *History of the East Kent Volunteers*, written and published in Ashford in 1899 by Charles Igglesden.

13

19th-Century Expansion

As was discussed in chapter 6, the 19th century saw a great increase in the population of Ashford. From about 2,000 in 1801 the total rose by about 50 per cent in the next 40 years, and then in the next 60 increased fourfold. This latter change was, of course, largely due to the opening of the railway works in 1847. The increase in Ashford during the first 40 years was less than that for Kent as a whole, for which the increase was nearly 75 per cent, but in the next 60 years the increase for Kent was only to double. For the whole of the century the population of Ashford increased to six times, whilst that for Kent only four times.

To accommodate this growing population there was obviously the need for much housing, particularly after 1850. The areas on either side of North Street and Canterbury Road, between New Street and the newly built Godinton Road were developed at this time. The most extensive expansion was in South Ashford, where, until the railway works were built, there were only farms and scattered cottages.

29. *A drawing of street entertainment, mid-19th century.*

Local Government   The growing population required better local administration, and as the century passed those services now thought essential to town living were either expanded or introduced for the first time.

Reference has already been made to the Improvement Commissioners, appointed from 1824 after a local Act of Parliament. They introduced the regular watching at night, the lighting of the streets (at first by oil lamps, but from 1832 by gas), and from 1845 the cleansing and watering of the streets—'sufficient to lay the dust'. They provided the first public convenience in 1861. They also took action to reduce nuisances—in 1836 notice was given to William Scott 'not to leave his waggon in the street for any longer time than necessary for loading and unloading', and George Reeve (a butcher) was ordered to abate the nuisance from his filthy blood hole and slaughterhouse. In order to finance their activities, the Commissioners had power to levy a rate.

The Commissioners were a select body. The first 28 were named in the Act, and as those ceased to be members because of death or other reason, the survivors had power to elect successors. A list of the members is given in Appendix XV. Although enthusiasm was

Radical Slavery!!

When OUT of Office 1904-5	When IN Office 1906-7
Ordinance Sanctioned by **Unionist** Government for Chinese in S. Africa **10 HOURS A DAY AT 11/= A WEEK** with Board and Lodging.	Convention Established by **Radical** Government for Blacks including **WOMEN & CHILDREN** in New Hebrides, **14 HOURS A DAY AT 2/6 A WEEK** with Board and Lodging.

Dont trust the Radicals again
with their "terminological inexactitudes," but
Support the Unionists

30.   *Elections were keenly contested in the Edwardian period. This leaflet was issued by the Conservative and Unionist party for the general election of 1908.*

probably high to begin with, this seems soon to have waned. In 1829 two members were disqualified, not having attended a meeting for 12 months. Between April and August 1843 eight meetings were called, but abandoned for want of a quorum, and from then onwards only a few meetings were held each year.

In 1863 the town decided to make a change. Following a meeting of inhabitants, it was agreed to adopt the provisions of the Local Government Act 1858, and to elect a local Board of Health. This was the first local body that can be described as democratically elected, although the franchise was limited. The new body first met on 1 May 1863, and continued until 1895. Its members are also listed in Appendix XV. The Board had wider powers than the Commissioners, and clearly thought that they should control all public activities. They clashed with the voluntary fire brigade, whose members did not see why they, who had existed as an organisation since the early part of the century, should be in any way directed by the Board.

Amongst the changes brought in by the Board was the requirement, from 1865, that all streets were to be named and houses numbered. They introduced in 1867 the collection

31.   This picture shows the crowd greeting the announcement of the election results in January 1910. Laurence Hardy, the conservative candidate, was re-elected. He was the member of parliament for Ashford from 1892-1918.

32.   *The fountain in Victoria park was presented by George Harper on 24 July 1912. The fountain was made in France, and first exhibited in 1862 at the 2nd International Exhibition in London. Afterwards it was purchased by Mr. Erle Drax for his house at Olantigh, near Wye which was destroyed by fire in 1903.*

33.   *Planting a memorial tree in Victoria park, 1910. In that and the following year 50 trees were planted to commemorate past and present townsmen, and five for Queen Victoria, King Edward, Queen Alexandra, King George and Queen Mary.*

34.   The lodge and entrance to the cemetery in Canterbury Road, opened by the Burial Board in 1860.

of household refuse. In 1872 they complained to the railway company of the 'inadequacy of third class accommodation, and the late arrival of goods trains'. In refusing to increase passenger accommodation the railway company gave as a reason that 'they contribute largely to the rates, have provided schools and pay a large sum for education, and subscribe to the church'. All no doubt true, but hardly relevant! The real reason was perhaps the view of Sir Edward Watkin, chairman of the railway company, who believed that it was in the financial interest of the company to provide very limited third-class accommodation, in the hope that intending passengers would be persuaded to buy second class.

The Board continued the work of the commissioners in suppressing nuisances. In 1866 they made orders in respect of 'Mr Blechynden's pig in the Glebe gardens', a nuisance 'in the shape of a Barrell for Pig Wash' at 15 Providence Street, and Mr Broad's tallow chandlers' works in Park Street. On the other hand the Board was much slower in dealing with a nuisance caused by them. The convenience (a urinal only, in the buildings of Middle Row) provided in 1861 was the subject of much complaint from 1869. The call for its closure was led by the partners of the Bank whose office, in the house where Lloyd's Bank is today, was very close to the offending convenience. Arguments as to the extent of the nuisance and over possible alternative sites went on for many years. Although some work was carried out, complaints continued. The Board had apparently underestimated the strength of the opposition, or the fact that they were not the freeholders of the site. In 1876 Robert Furley, who had acquired the whole building from the lord of the manor, gave the Board notice to quit, and the convenience was closed. The argument did not end there. For a further three years there was controversy as to the payment of rent, and the terms under which the Board should be allowed to recover their property. During the 13 years that the facility was provided, the total expenditure of the Board on rent, water, lighting and repairs was £83 3s. 0d. The cost of closing, including the legal expenses, was £106 16s. 5d.

35. The cemetery in 1868. It was the custom for townspeople to use the cemetery as a public open space, strolling round to admire the planting and the graves.

An interesting insight into administrative efficiency is given by one aspect of the argument. On 2 January 1878 the Board agreed to ask the Local Government Board in London for power to acquire the site compulsorily. The public enquiry was held on 16 February—a Saturday—and the result was reported to the Board at their meeting on 6 March! From time to time the question of applying for a charter of incorporation as a Borough was considered. No action was ever taken on this issue.

Other activities of the Board included the provision of playing fields in 1886 (now Victoria Park), although the land was at first only leased from the Jemmett family, who were the owners. When the question of a swimming bath was raised in 1867, the Board suggested that this should be provided by a private company. They agreed to help by contributing £10 a year towards establishment charges, until such time as the company was able to pay four per cent interest on its capital. The pool was built in Beaver Road on land leased from the Jemmetts. The Board took over in 1891. The sites of the pool and the park were purchased by the Urban District Council in 1898.

The burial of the dead was entirely a church matter until 1859. For centuries the place of burial was the churchyard, or (for the privileged few who could pay high fees) in the church. The great increase in numbers during the period that many troops were in the town made these arrangements insufficient—there were over 900 burials in the years 1800-9, about three times the previous level. A new burial ground was provided by the Vestry in 1800 on about half an acre of land, owned by the vicar, fronting Station Road. When this ground was becoming full, a Burial Board was established which opened the new burial ground in Canterbury Road in 1859. Although legally separate from the Local Board, many members and officers were common to both bodies. The powers of the Burial Board were absorbed by the Urban District Council from 1 April 1900. The cemetery at Bybrook was acquired in 1906.

Local Boards were abolished by the Local Government Act, 1894. Elections were held in Ashford on 17 December, and the first meeting of the successor body, the Urban District Council, was held on 2 January 1895. Mr. W.G. Handcock, the last chairman of the Board, was elected to be the first chairman of the Urban District.

Post   A public service that was greatly extended in the 19th century was that of the post. The General Post Office had been introduced in 1660, and developed gradually over the years. By 1840 a regular service was provided, covering most parts of the country. Charges were based on the distance involved, and in the 19th century were as follows:

	not exceeding	8 miles	2d.
		30 miles	6d.
		15 miles	4d.
		50 miles	7d.
		20 miles	5d.
		80 miles	8d.

In 1840 the standard charge of 1d., prepaid by adhesive stamps, was introduced.

36.   *A view of the lower High Street at the beginning of this century. The shop occupied by Alexander, 41 & 43 High Street, was the post office of John Tunbridge from about 1818 until 1861. The drinking fountain was presented by Robert Furley in 1864.*

Ashford was made a post town in June 1675, when Robert Lott was appointed post-master. He was to be paid 20 per cent of postages as salary, but this proved to be so low that an additional payment was authorised in 1677. At the same time there were complaints of neglect by the postmaster who was only collecting the mail once a week—whether this was the cause or effect of the low receipts and therefore salary is not known. Troubles continued—in 1687 the Treasury recorded that £2 8s. 6d. due from the Ashford post-master, Robert Lott, was not likely to be recovered, as he had 'run away'.

All post at this time was carried by postboys on horseback, and came to Ashford from London via Maidstone and Lenham, three times a week. This continued until May 1817, when a daily post was introduced.

A major consideration during the second half of the 18th century was that of security. Indeed, conditions were so bad that the official advice to those wishing to send banknotes by post was to cut them in half, and send them by separate posts. The solution from 1770 was to replace postboys by mail carts, and in 1784 to introduce mail coaches. These were proposed by John Palmer of Bath: they carried an iron safe for keeping the mail, as well as armed guards. By 1790 these were in use on all main post routes.

In 1830 it was decided to bring the Ashford mail from London to Canterbury by mail coach, and from there by postboy. The post office records show that this 'boy' was armed in order to defend the mails if he were attacked.

From less than £60 in 1685, postage revenues increased in the 18th century—in 1730 they were £163, but declined to £125 in 1750. The names of most of the postmasters are known, and some details of them and their premises are given in Appendix XVI. Since one of the duties of a postmaster was to provide horses for the postmen, innkeepers were commonly holders of the position.

37.   *View of the lower High Street looking east in 1868.*

The post office was moved to 2 Bank Street (the building is now a branch of National Westminster Bank), a new house built for the postmaster, John Munns. The site was owned by the Church, being part of that given by Sir John Fogge, and Munns took a 99-year-lease at £9 a year. The new office was opened on 3 January 1870, and was used until the present building in Tufton Street was opened on 2 April 1921.

Linked with the post office was the telephone service. This was started in Ashford about 1896 by the National Telephone Company. The first exchange was in Middle Row, and the directory for 1897 listed nine subscribers. The undertaking (with 61 other exchanges nationwide) was transferred to the Post Office from 1 January 1912.

Gas   The first of the modern public utilities to be provided was a gas supply. The invention or discovery of the use of coal gas as a means of lighting was made by William Murdock. He was employed by Boulton and Watt, and lit their factory at Soho in Birmingham in 1802. The first gas company was the Gas Light and Coke Company incorporated by an Act of Parliament in 1812, which provided gas for the Westminster area of London. By 1820 most of the larger cities had a gas supply.

The first works in Ashford were built in Station Road (just below St John's Lane) in 1832. In that year John Bryan of Maidstone, describing himself as a 'gas contractor', bought the land and agreed with the Commissioners that 42 lamps should be erected and lit with gas. In 1833 the undertaking was purchased by William Beck Hills, described as previously of Maidstone but then of Ashford, in association with Thomas Hills of Thurnham, Walter Hills of Chatham and Walter Hills and Robert Hazell, both of Maidstone. Hills offered to sell the undertaking to the Commissioners for £6,000, but they declined. In 1865 a limited company was formed, with a share capital of £20,000, of which only £13,800 was issued. The undertaking became extremely profitable in later years, paying a dividend of 7½ per cent in 1886, rising to 10 per cent by 1894. In addition a bonus of 30 per cent was paid in 1895! One of the reasons for this profitability was that the company refused to extend the mains to the newer parts of the town in the expansion from 1850, without the Local Board making a contribution (usually 50 per cent) towards the cost. New gas works were built south of the railway in 1868.

There were many complaints over the years about the quality of the gas supply. It was said that the gas was impure, and caused discoloration of the walls of the rooms in which it was burnt, and that (particularly in South Ashford) the pressure was so low that it was impossible to obtain a good light. So bad was the position that in 1865, when there was a dispute over whether a contribution should be made towards the cost of new mains, there was a proposal to start a separate company to supply South Ashford. The railway company had decided not to take supplies from the town works, but erected their own in 1850.

In December 1893 the Local Board decided to acquire the undertaking. The company replied that they did not wish to sell, and the Board decided not to proceed at that time, apparently being influenced by the fact that the Chairman of the directors, Mr. J.U. Bugler, who had been chairman of the Board and a county councillor, was strongly opposed to the take-over. The newly elected Urban District Council had no such inhibitions. In December 1895 their Clerk wrote to the Secretary of the Company, expressing the wish of the Council to open negotiations for purchase. In the exchange of letters that followed, it was clear that agreement was not possible. In July 1896 Mr. F. Hughes-Hallett wrote 'that it would be more to his taste to withdraw for the present from advising the Gas Company'. Since he held both that post and that of Clerk to the Council, it was obvious that his position was difficult!

After further meetings and correspondence, the Council called a public meeting in July 1897 to get support for the promotion of a Bill in Parliament. Feelings were running high—Elisha Davies (a shareholder of the Gas Company, and a partner in Ashford Bank) sent a circular to all shareholders urging them to attend the meeting and oppose the Council. Since 58 out of 121 shareholders lived outside the district, it is likely that only a few were present at the meeting. On the other hand, the Council issued a handbill seeking support, and there were said to be 700–800 people present. When the vote was taken only about six opposed the Council.

To counter the Council's action the Company also promoted a Parliamentary Bill. This was intended to give them statutory powers to operate, something they had never possessed. They had operated since 1832, including the digging up of roads to lay mains without any authority whatsoever. This, and the long history of complaints against the company by the public without action by the Local Board, was attributed by several who gave evidence to the Parliamentary enquiry to the fact that for many years several persons had been members, and even chairmen, of both the Board and the Gas Company.

Eventually Parliament approved the Council's application, and the power to purchase compulsorily was granted in 1897. The purchase price was determined by arbitrators at £34,080, being 22 years' purchase of the profits—a very generous multiplier, particularly when the large contributions made by the Board towards the laying of mains is taken into account.

Water   The position on water supply was in many respects the direct opposite to that of the gas undertaking. In this case the Company was anxious to sell, but the Board refused.

Until the middle of the 19th century townspeople relied on such wells as they dug within their own boundaries, or on the town pump in the High Street, which was maintained by the local authority. It is typical of the great care taken by the Board to avoid spending that, when the pump was renewed in 1868, they saved 10 shillings by requiring that the old handle should be used.

The date of the first piped supply is not known, but in 1854 a private water supply company was registered under the Companies Act. This must have formalised an earlier arrangement, since a report on possible alternative supplies to that obtained from the river at the mill in East Hill was made in 1852. The property of that company was transferred to a new limited liability company for £2,037 in 1869.

The 1852 report strongly recommended that water should be obtained from a well sunk in land, owned by the parish for charitable purposes, at Black Forstall in Challock. It was said that an adequate supply of extremely good water could be obtained and, since it was considerably higher than the town, there would be no difficulty in distribution. The recommendation was not accepted, presumably on grounds of cost, despite the many criticisms of the current supply drawn from the river.

38.   View of the lower High Street looking west, with the town pump, at the beginning of this century.

In 1866 the Company asked the Board to acquire the water undertaking and 'to supply the Town with a purer and more wholesome water'. The Board declined, saying that 'they had not enough evidence to warrant such an outlay'. The supply at that time was not continuous, and the Board ordered in 1867 that notice of a fire should be given to the police, and they would contact Mr. King (the waterworks manager) at the mill to arrange for the pumps 'to go to work'. A continuous supply was provided from August 1892.

A further report was made in this year by the same consulting engineer, Mr. Samuel Collett Homersham, who had made the 1852 report. He repeated his advice to obtain water from Black Forstall, but this was again rejected. In 1871 the Company acquired rights to search for and extract water from land on the boundary of Ashford and Willesborough, at Henwood.

In 1880 the question of the town's acquisition of the works was raised again. On this occasion Mr. Bugler was apparently in favour, and resigned as chairman when the matter was opposed (but he was persuaded to withdraw his resignation). However in the following year the Board changed its mind, and the undertaking was bought for £10,722.

After the purchase from Lord Hothfield of land at Barrow Hill in 1882 for a reservoir, the water undertaking was continued by the Board, and then by the Council.

Sewerage and Sewage Disposal   For many centuries the townspeople had no means of disposing of waste liquids other than into cesspits or in the High Street by the town gutter. This ran from Middle Row down (on what was probably the original line of the frontage, but by the 16th century was at the back of the buildings) to Marsh Lane (now Station Road), from where the water found its way to the river. The gutter was probably a shallow depression, either brick- or stone-lined, and for many centuries it marked the boundary on the south side of the High Street between freehold and copyhold land. The Sewer Commissioners, responsible for regulating the river, ordered the placing of a grating to 'stay the sullage that comes from Ashford Town into the main river' in 1606, so that there was a problem even then, with a population perhaps only one-tenth of that in the latter part of the 19th century.

From 1863 onward some sewers were provided but, in the absence of any disposal system, these still drained into the nearest watercourse, and from there eventually into the river. Even when the Local Board agreed to the provision of sewers, delays occurred in their construction, as in September 1865 when the surveyor reported that he had been unable to start work in Dover Place because all the labourers had gone hopping!

There can be no doubt of the effect this had on the water supply. The report made in 1866 said, 'the surface of the ground slopes in a gradual inclination from the top of Ashford down to the well [at the Mill] and the ground for this distance for a considerable breadth is covered with an almost continuous line of inhabited houses, mostly having cesspools or drains, the source of the impurity in the water is plainly apparent'.

Despite this and the outbreak of cholera and other diseases, the town was for a long time opposed to the building of sewage works. Eventually, in 1870, after a letter from the Medical Committee of the Privy Council regarding fever in the town, and after long discussions as to the relative merits and costs of several surveyors, the Board appointed Mr. Baldwin Latham to report on a new system. When the report was received a town meeting was called to consider whether action should be taken. At this meeting on 2 November 1870, a resolution was passed expressing the opinion that the drainage was satisfactory, and was not injurious to health, despite the statement that between July and

September of that year there had been 84 deaths in the parish, including 25 from scarlet fever and 10 from typhoid. At a subsequent meeting the Board decided to defer action on new works, but authorised the construction of three cesspools to reduce pollution in the river. At their meeting on 4 January 1871 they accepted the resolution passed at the public meeting, and went on to make decisions on more pressing matters—prosecutions for using obscene language, and for sliding in the street!

The attitude of the Board towards public health can be seen in 1873 when, despite pressure from the Board of Health in London, they refused to appoint a Medical Officer of Health. When Mr. William Sheppard was finally appointed in December 1873, one of his first reports was to declare the water in South Ashford unfit for drinking. In August 1874 there were complaints that the river was polluted, and it was agreed that the river bed at Mill Bridge should be cleansed.

So the matter went on, with frequent requests from the Local Government Board in London for a report on progress—so regularly that there was laughter at the meeting on 8 September 1877 when it was reported that no letter had been received during the previous month. In 1876 a private resident (later identified as William Burra, a partner of Ashford Bank) offered to give £2,000 towards the cost of providing efficient drainage. The Board asked for reports from a Mr. Mansergh, and he was instructed to prepare plans. The Board visited Aylesbury in 1877, and Aldershot, Eltham and Windsor in 1878 to see their sewerage system. In 1880 they went to Hertford, and in this year positive progress was made. The Board applied for, and had approved, the compulsory purchase of land at Bybrook for the sewage disposal works. But still no works. In 1882 they went to Eastbourne, and in 1883 were seeking the advice of Mr. Isaac Shone of Wrexham. Mr. Bugler resigned his membership (as he had in 1879 over the question of purchasing the water undertaking), as he was in a minority in the sewerage question, and again was persuaded to withdraw his resignation.

Several members of the Board clearly considered themselves greater experts on the means of disposing of sewage than their engineer, and put forward suggestions to solve the problem at far less cost. Eventually, in 1883, the Board dispensed with the services of Mansergh, despite having paid him substantial sums in fees and expenses. During these years some progress was made in the construction of sewers, but still they drained into the river. Complaints were made in 1884 by the Commissioners for Sewers (the river authority), and in 1885 they issued a writ against the Board for polluting the river.

The feeling in the town was expressed in an editorial in the *Kentish Express* for 4 October 1884:

> The public of Kent will soon begin to think they have heard more than enough of the Ashford Sewerage Question ... Judging by the proposal of Wednesday night, one might almost be inclined to fancy that a portion of the Board would not think the prospect of this flow of controversial eloquence going on indefinitely altogether a calamitous one. But, of course every one of them is in earnest. Nothing is further from their thoughts than the idea of trifling with the question. They all intend to delay no longer when that principle, and those plans come before them which are, beyond disputation, perfect.

In November 1884 a new scheme was submitted by Edmund Ballard, a surveyor, and partner in Ashford with A.J. Burrows, a surveyor and estate agent. In August 1885 the Board accepted this scheme, now put forward by Ballard in conjunction with Jones, an engineer of Ealing. The town displayed no surprise that a decision had now been reached, since Ballard was the son-in-law of Bugler, the Chairman of the Board!

Eventually, on 7 September 1887, the tender of Mr. G.A. Wallis of Maidstone was accepted for sewage works at a contract price of £6,180. The whole story was summarised in the editorial of the *Kentish Express* for 10 September 1887, in which they commented 'in the debate of 4 January 1865 ... the view of Mr. Whitfeld was that Ashford should wait, to profit by the experience of other towns, before adopting any plan for preventing the pollution of the river. It cannot be said that the advice has not been followed'. The paper estimated the total cost of the abandoned plans and legal expenses at £2,500. The new works came into operation early in 1889.

Electricity   There was no public supply of electricity in Ashford until 1926, although there was a long period of 19th-century non-development, an even longer period of discussion than with the provision of sewage works!

The matter was first raised in 1882, the year of the first Act of Parliament governing the supply of electricity. Notice was received by the Board that two private companies intended to apply for Parliamentary powers to supply electricity. The Board resolved to oppose the applications, and to apply for powers themselves. Nothing more is recorded of this decision.

In 1892 the Chairman and one other member of the Board proposed that a report should be prepared on the advisability of applying for permission themselves, but nothing was done. In 1894 another company gave notice. The Board resolved that the Clerk should make further enquiries, 'with a view to blocking the intentions of the company as far as possible', and again nothing more happened.

History repeated itself in 1898, when yet another company was involved. The Council opposed and made application themselves, and on this occasion did proceed to obtain powers by a Provisional Order, confirmed by an Act of Parliament (62-63 Victoria *c*.CXX). This allowed for a very limited distribution system, as mains were to be laid within two years in the following streets: North Street as far north as the junction with Hardinge Road, High Street from Castle Street to Marsh Lane (Station Road), Bank Street and Elwick Road, Beaver Road as far as Christ Church. But nothing was done to provide the works, and the subsequent events are detailed in the next chapter.

Some premises did have a private supply long before this date. When giving evidence in favour of the Council acquiring the gas undertaking in 1897, Mr. L. Pledge, the senior partner in the milling firm of H.S. Pledge & Sons, said that their factory was lit by electricity generated on the site. He stated that this was necessary because of the deficiencies in the gas supply. Within the next decade other businesses (including the two cinemas) were providing their own supply, generated by gas engines using the town gas supply. The railway works had a private system from 1912.

Fire Brigade   There was probably a voluntary fire brigade in Ashford from 1814, but there are few records before 1826. In that year a meeting was held in the Vestry Room to consider making 'some regulations for the better management of the Fire Engine belonging to the Parish'. It was believed for many years that this was the first volunteer fire brigade in the country, but more recent research shows that this honour belongs to Hythe, whose association was formed in 1802. (See the book by Harry Klopper, *To Fire Committed: the History of Fire Fighting in Kent*, 1984.)

It is fortunate that a very full record of the brigade and of notable fires is available, in a history written in 1913 by H. Wood and the then captain of the brigade, F.S. Hart. This has recently been reprinted, with additions to 1942, by A.E.W. Palmer. At that date the

39. *(top) Lord Mount-Charles, who was the tenant of Godinton c.1860, was a keen amateur fireman and formed his own private brigade. They worked with the Ashford brigade, and this picture shows the two engines at Godinton.*

40. *(above) The brigade with the 'steamer' engine, outside the fire station in Middle Row, 1919.*

41. *(right) The brigade relied on voluntary contributions from tradesmen and others for its support. This picture shows the collector, Mr. J.F. Worger, on his round.*

42. *The brigade entered many competitions, and this picture shows the captain and chief officers. The cup is that awarded as runner-up in the Fire Brigade Union championship held in Agricultural Hall, London in June 1896.*

brigade was absorbed into the war-time National Fire Service, and after the war transferred to the control of the County Council.

The early fire brigades derived much of their support from the insurance companies—indeed it is probably no coincidence that the Hythe brigade was formed in the same year as the Kent Fire Office. In some towns (not in Ashford) brigades were maintained by the insurance companies, and would only deal with fires in premises in which they had an interest, as shown by 'fire plates' fixed to the outside wall. One still exists in Ashford, affixed to the wall of 4 Middle Row.

The Ashford brigade was financed by the subscriptions of those who were members of the Association, and by charges to others if the brigade attended fires at their premises. The Ashford brigade provided assistance not only in the case of fires in the town, but also over a wide stretch of the surrounding countryside. A summary of the more extensive fires that occurred is given in Appendix XV.

About 1814 a station to house the engines was provided (free of charge to the brigade) at the rear of the workhouse in Gravel Walk. When the workhouse was sold, following the introduction of the Union workhouse at Hothfield in 1836, the fire engine was moved to new premises adjoining Gravel Walk. As has been mentioned, the Local Board, when

43.   More views of the fire brigade. This one shows the captain using less formal transport!

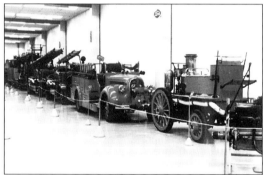

44.   The brigade always took part in town parades, this one in 1910.

45.   This old Ashford engine, fully restored, is now exhibited in the Southward museum at Paraparaumu, New Zealand.

elected in 1863, thought that it ought to have control over all public services in the town, and this led to a clash with the fire brigade. The minutes of the Board record in 1864 'that the means of firefighting should be discussed with the brigade'. In 1867 the board purchased land in Park Street for a depot for tools etc., and suggested that the engines should be housed there. This was rejected by the brigade. There was, however, some co-operation. In 1871 the Board agreed to fix a fire brigade lamp to a post outside the house of Walter Hill (engineer to the brigade) in New Street, and the following year it was agreed that the fire escape should be kept on waste land owned by G.A. Lewis (of Lewis & Hyland) in Gilbert Road. In 1876 the engines were moved to new premises at 24 New

Street. In 1893 these premises were required by the owner and, after some negotiations with the Board and the District Council, new premises were provided in Middle Row. At the same time a trust was formed to own the equipment of the brigade, the members being the Chairman of the Council, the chief officer of the brigade, and two others.

The brigade achieved a high level of efficiency, and entered many competitions. In 1896 they were the champions of the South East, and therefore represented the area in the finals of the national competition. They reached the final round, only narrowly being beaten. Fuller details of the brigade, its members and the larger fires can be found in the book already referred to.

Banking   The first bank to operate in Ashford was formed in 1791. The members were the brothers George and William Jemmett (known as 'Gold' and 'Silver' Jemmett), and Lewis Whitfeld, their title being Messrs. Jemmett, Whitfeld and Jemmett. Members of the Jemmett family, with other partners, continued to own the bank until 1902 when the business was sold to Lloyds Bank.

In 1833 Virgil Pomfret became a partner with William Jemmett, son of George. In 1848 the partnership comprised George Elwick Jemmett (grandson of the first George), Pomfret, William Burra and Edward Simmonds. The Burra and Pomfret families (who were related by marriage) seem to have acquired the major interest, since in 1875 the name of the bank became Pomfret & Co. The Jemmetts were still involved, the last manager of the local bank and the first manager for the branch of Lloyds being William Francis Bond Jemmett. The family owned much land in south Ashford, and his name is given to streets in the area.

The bank was probably first opened in the house of George Jemmett on East Hill (now called Nightingale House, part of Ashford school), but within a year or two moved to premises owned by Lewis Whitfeld, one of the partners, in the building which is now 24 North Street. By 1798 it was established in premises owned by the Church, now 83 High Street (on the west corner with Bank Street). In the church records for 1842 that building is described as the 'old Bank', and the bank was in the house of George Elwick Jemmett on the site where it is now. The present building was opened on 28 July 1926. Fuller details of Ashford Bank and of the partners can be found in the article by the present author in *Bygone Kent* for July 1992, vol. 12, p.432.

The next bank to be opened in the town was opened on 1 February 1810. It would seem to have been on a small scale, and little is known of it apart from its name— Ashford Commercial Bank, and the names of the original partners, Messrs. de Lasaux, Haffenden, Hutton and Boghurst. It was closed by 1829. About 1840 a branch of the

ASHFORD BANK,

ASHFORD, KENT, 30th June, 1902.

DEAR

We beg to inform you that, in consequence of arrangements entered into between LLOYDS BANK LIMITED and ourselves, the business of our Firm will be amalgamated with that Bank on the 1st July next.

We desire to thank you and our customers for the great kindness which has so very generally been accorded to us, and for the confidence and support which the Firm has received since the establishment of the Bank in 1791; and we cordially recommend our successors to you, being assured that you will meet with every attention and consideration at their hands.

They have taken over our existing staff, and there will be no break in the conduct of business at our present premises.

All the members of our Firm will be interested in the Bank after the transfer, and Mr. JEMMETT will continue to take an active part in the supervision of the local business.

We are, dear

Yours faithfully,

POMFRET, BURRA & CO.

46.   *The letter sent to all customers in 1902 by the Ashford Bank of Pomfret, Burra & Co., announcing the amalgamation of that bank with Lloyds Bank Ltd.*

London and County Bank was opened in the lower High Street (now no. 20). This is today a branch of National Westminster Bank.

About 1905 a branch of the Capital and Counties Bank was opened at 22 Bank Street. This bank was merged with Lloyds Bank in 1922, and continued as a branch of that bank until closed in 1926. The National Provincial Bank opened a branch in the old post office in Bank Street in 1923—this is today another branch of the National Westminster Bank.

The Trustee savings Bank movement started in Scotland around the beginning of the 19th century. The intention was to provide facilities for the poorer classes to save at times when they had a little more income. The hope was that, by doing so, they would be able to manage at times of low income, without recourse to poor relief.

The Ashford bank was founded on 1 September 1816 as the 'Ashford Provident Society, for securing the Savings of Tradesmen, Mechanic Labourer, Servant, Industrious Poor and their children, living in the Town of Ashford or parishes adjacent'. It was one of the very earliest in the country, since the standard history of the banks names only seven as having opened in early years. The first president was the Earl of Thanet, with 23 eminent local gentlemen as the first trustees. Messrs. Charles Stoddart and Henry Creed were joint secretaries, with Mr. Stephen Tournay as clerk. The principles of the bank can be seen from the limitation on deposits—£100 in the first year, and not more than £50 in subsequent years. In 1820 it was resolved that, in future, applications for accounts 'from Gentlemen, Ladies or Opulent Tradesmen and Farmers (or their children)' should not be dealt with by the secretary, but referred to the Committee. For many years it was carried on at 25 High Street. By 1841 it had 920 depositors, and total funds of £33,110. Like many other trustee banks, it was badly affected by the Post Office Savings Bank, opened in 1861, and by increasing control by Parliament. This was intended to prevent the repetition of failures and misappropriations, and also to secure the investment of surpluses in the Treasury. There was also increasing complaint by the commercial banks of what they regarded as unfair competition. Following an Act of Parliament in 1891 which introduced greater control, the Ashford Bank was closed. The present trustee bank is the successor to a branch of the Brighton Bank, opened in 1947.

A Penny Bank was opened in Ashford on 1 January 1859. This bank was similar in many ways to the trustee bank, but accepted deposits of one penny (hence its name), whereas the trustee bank had a minimum of one shilling. The bank in Ashford was run by the same persons and from the same premises as the trustee bank. It closed at the same time.

Markets   The development of markets from very early times has already been described. In the last century there was increasing concern about the problems caused by this being held in the lower High Street. This was a cause of annoyance to townspeople not on market business, while it was also too small for the growing volume of trade.

Accordingly, a meeting of graziers and agriculturists was held on 8 January 1856. Following a public meeting in the *Saracen's Head* on 26 February, a public company was formed, with a capital of £2,500. The site of about five acres was leased from George Elwick Jemmett for 99 years, with an option to purchase. Jemmett, as lord of the manor of Ashford, also sold all the market rights of the manor. The market company exercised their right to purchase in 1868.

The new site was first used on 17 May 1856, for the May Fair. This was the fair granted by charter to St Stephen's Chapel in 1466, the date being amended from 6 May by the

47. *The Corn Exchange in Bank Street, erected in 1861. It was used not only for the sale of corn, etc., but for all manner of public performances and entertainments. It was demolished in the 1970s.*

adoption of the Gregorian calendar in 1752. The first general market was held on the site on 29 July 1856, and a commemoration dinner for about two hundred and fifty people was held in the High Street at 4 p.m. on that day. Before trading could take place, lots were drawn to determine positions. Mr. Daniel Chittenden, as the oldest salesman from the Marsh, drew for the Marshmen, and Mr. Charles Small, the oldest on the Hill, for the Hillmen. The result was Marshmen on the west, Hillmen on the east.

The market was held on the first and third Tuesdays in each month. Representations were made for this to be altered to alternate Tuesdays, because of a clash with Rye market. Several attempts were made, but neither Ashford nor Rye would agree to a change. The position remained unaltered until 27 June 1865, from which date the Ashford market was held weekly. Another celebration dinner was held to mark the occasion, this time in the *Saracen's Head*. The market has been held on this same site weekly ever since, but it is now proposed to move to an out-of-town site.

The practice of selling corn by sample, rather than in bulk, was well established by the early 19th century. For a time there were two rival corn markets—one in the *Royal Oak* inn, and the other in the public rooms in Middle Row. This latter became the more important.

Increasing demand for space, and the moving of the general market to the new site led to proposals for a new corn exchange. A new company was formed in 1861, and it was suggested that the old market might continue in the afternoon, with the new market operating in the morning.

The new corn exchange was built at the lower end of Bank street, and was used not only for the corn market but for all manner of public entertainments and exhibitions until it was demolished in the 1970s and an office block built in the site.

Newspapers   The number of newspapers, and their circulation, was restricted by the imposition of a tax on advertisements and a stamp duty. These were not repealed until 1853 and 1855 respectively, and from this date the number of papers increased.

The usual newspapers for items relating to Ashford were those published in Canterbury. These included the *Kentish Post*, from 1717 to 1838, and the *Kentish Gazette*, from 1768. Also used were the Maidstone-based *Maidstone Journal*, from 1786 to 1911, the *Kentish Gazette*, from 1815, and the *Kent Messenger*, from 1859.

The first Ashford paper was the short lived *Ashford Advertiser and Illustrated Peoples Paper*, published from August 1854 to July 1855. In that year the *Kentish Express* and *Alfred News* were produced, the first being dated 14 July 1855. 'Alfred' was the name given originally by the railway company to their development, but this was soon dropped in favour of 'Newtown'. This paper, whose founder-editor was Henry Igglesden, was the pioneer penny paper in Kent, and by the end of the century had achieved a wide circulation throughout east Kent.

About 1884 another newspaper was started in Ashford: the *Kent Examiner and Ashford Chronicle*. There is some doubt as to the precise date since no copies of the paper for the first three years are known to exist. The original publishers were Headley, but within a few years the Boorman family were

48.   Henry Igglesden was born in Dover in 1826, but came to Ashford in 1848 to start a stationery and printing business. In 1855 he founded the first penny paper in Kent, which later became the Kentish Express.

associated with it. The successors to that firm now publish both the *Kent Messenger* and the *Kentish Express*, the result of a merger between the companies.

The only other Ashford paper known at this period is the short lived *Ashford Guardian*, issued from September 1868 to January 1869.

14

The Last 90 Years

The pace of change has accelerated in this century, both because of the technological changes that affect everywhere, but also because of important developments that have particularly concerned Ashford. The volume and complexity of the changes mean that it is not possible to cover all subjects here—the exclusion of some will perhaps disappoint some readers.

On several occasions there have been proposals for the substantial expansion of the town. In 1900 the railway company was considering a new railway station, and discussions took place with the Council for this to be built at the bottom end of Bank Street, with a road bridge to give a new access to the town from the south. At much the same time a proposal was made for the building of a new road to link Elwick Road to Hythe Road. Neither of these proposals was realised.

In 1909 a scheme was launched for the building of Ashford Garden City. A company was registered under the Industrial and Provident Societies Act 1893 with the intention of creating a co-operative ownership scheme, on the lines of Letchworth, Hampstead and

49.   *View of the lower High Street looking north at the beginning of this century.*

50.   View of the lower High Street, the north side, near to the junction with Station road, about 1905.

51.   The same view, some twenty years later.

Bournville. The Ashford scheme, at least in the original prospectus, was much smaller, consisting of about three hundred houses on land south of Hythe road, almost on the parish boundary. In the event the scheme did not succeed, and eventually the land was sold, and the town football ground and the North senior schools were built there.

Economic conditions between the wars did not favour large scale expansion, but after the last war the government considered that there was a need for substantial growth outside the major urban areas. A report in 1947 by Professor Patrick Abercrombie on the London area stated that 'of the Kent towns within reasonable distance of London, only Ashford is suitable for industrial expansion; it is a good distribution centre'. The County Council, as

52.   A view of the new housing development in Canterbury Road, taken about 1910.

planning authority, agreed with this conclusion, and suggested expansion to a population of 40,000. The first action by the government was the passing of the New Towns Act 1947, under which development commissions were set up to build several new towns in the counties surrounding London. Ashford was not included, but discussions in about 1950 concluded that expansion should be achieved by different means. It was apparently thought that the New Town Commissions were not suited to the expansion of a sizeable existing town, although the population of Ashford was very similar to that of Hemel Hempstead, which was developed by that means. In 1952 the government passed the Town Development Act, to cater for the needs of expansion in towns like Ashford.

Locally the proposal was debated for some years. On one side it was argued that there was a need to introduce new industry, since it was feared that the railway works (still by far the largest employer in the town) would be closed. Against this there was concern by those who did not want to see the market town character of the town destroyed. The controversy became largely political, and was debated back and forth for years. Not until the Labour party gained control of the Urban Council in 1957 was a decision taken to proceed. In September 1959 an agreement was signed with the London County Council to build a total of 5,000 houses over a period of 15 years, of which 4,250 would be for persons coming from the London area, the balance being for local residents. Provision was made for the creation of industrial estates to provide employment for the newcomers. Financial help was given by the London County Council in addition to the government grants available for house building. This scheme has resulted in the building of substantial numbers of houses, although the changing pattern of house ownership has meant that the total envisaged to be built by the local authority has not been realised. Nevertheless, the agreement was a major reason for the increase in population of the town since the last war.

Government forecasts of national population increase by the end of the century, still showed that expansion was required to provide the necessary housing. In 1967 Professor Colin Buchanan was asked to investigate the possibility of a planned intake of 150,000 people over a period of 15 years. His report recommended designation under the New Towns Act, 1965 of an area that could accommodate in total a population of 240,000 by 1991—a new city rather than a town. However, before any action could be taken the government statisticians were realising that the high birth rate of the immediate post war years would not be permanent, and the need for expansion in the south east would be on a smaller scale. In 1968 the government announced that they would not proceed with the proposal for a new town in the Ashford area, but expansion on a more limited scale would continue.

Local Government   The Urban District had been formed in 1894, and the area was substantially increased by the inclusion, under the Kent Review Order 1934, of the parishes of Kennington and Willesborough, previously part of East Ashford Rural District. As a result the population increased from 15,248 to 22,099 and the area from some 2,800 acres to about twice that figure. In 1974, as a result of the Local Government Act of 1972, the urban district was merged with the borough of Tenterden, and the rural districts of East and West Ashford and Tenterden. The area is now 143,458 acres, and the present population about 95,000. In order that the additional area could be properly represented, the number of councillors was increased from 18 to 24 in 1934. From 1974 the new council has had 49 members.

After its formation, the Urban District Council implemented a number of schemes to improve the town. As has been said, the gas undertaking was acquired from a private company, as was the swimming bath. Land was bought for Victoria Park. In 1898 a water tower and reservoir were provided at Barrow Hill, and in 1901 new wells were constructed at Henwood to provide a new and better supply of water. In 1936 a new reservoir was built near Potters Corner.

In 1957 an agreement was made with the Mid Kent Water Company to contribute towards the cost of developing a new supply at Godmersham. In 1963 it was agreed that the undertaking should be sold to The Mid Kent Company, the purchase price to be £358,000 as at 1 April 1963. Objections to the sale meant that a public enquiry was necessary. The transfer was finally made on 1 October 1964, with an additional £15,577 being paid to the Council for capital expenditure incurred during the intervening 18 months.

New filter beds were provided at the sewage disposal works at a cost of £75,000 in 1928. The works then continued without major change until 1960, when the greatly increased flow caused overloading of the works, and many complaints from the public of the offensive smells. New works, necessary to cater for the London expansion scheme and for the disposal of industrial wastes, were started, and officially opened on 28 April 1965.

53.   A view of Ashford taken from the south-east, about 1930, with the railway works prominent in the foreground.
54.   The members and chief officers of the Urban District Council, taken just before its abolition in 1974.

55 & 56.   The badge or arms of the Ashford U.D.C. (from 1894 to 1974), and the arms of the new borough formed in 1974.

The saga of the provision of a public electricity supply ran even longer than that for the provision of proper sewage works. As has already been stated, the first occasion that the question was raised was in 1882, when a proposal was made by private companies. The Local Board opposed these plans, and resolved to apply for powers to allow them to undertake the supply. Nothing but discussion ensued until 1898, when the Urban Council, prompted by the notice of intention by other private companies, finally applied to Parliament for powers. These were granted by a Provisional Order, confirmed by an Act of Parliament in 1899. Again, nothing was done until 1901, when the powers were about to expire. An engineer was engaged, and a plan to supply on a low tension, three-wire system approved. Work did not start, and in February 1903 the Council decided to abandon the scheme. A month later it was reported that a local private company, the Ashford & District Electric Power Co., was being formed. The Council agreed not to oppose this company, who clearly found the costs greater than anticipated. In 1906 the company asked the Council to bear the cost of re-instating the roads after the laying of the cables—this was refused. In 1908 the Board of Trade revoked the powers of the company, since they had not complied with the conditions of the Order. In 1910 the East Kent Electric Supply Co. applied for powers to supply in Ashford, but, although the company was given the necessary parliamentary powers in the following year, nothing came of the proposal. In November 1914 the Board of Trade revoked the Order, since the company was not in a position to operate the undertaking. Not until 1923 did the Council take action, and in December 1925 powers were granted to the Council by Special Order. On this occasion work was actually started, the works being completed by October 1926, 44 years after the first proposals had been made. Electricity was used for the first time on the occasion of the visit by the Duke and Duchess of York to open the new hospital, when coloured lighting at the station was illuminated by the new system. The public supply was available from 1 November.

In order to provide for burials when the cemetery in Canterbury Road was full, the Council in 1902 purchased land at Burton farm, Kennington for a new cemetery. This proposal was frustrated by the owner of adjoining land building houses. After the Council had considered sites in Warren Lane, Victoria Park and Beaver, it was eventually decided to buy the 22 acres of land at Bybrook still in use as a cemetery from James S. Burra, at

57. *The western end of the market buildings. The shops replaced the old fish market in the early 19th century.*

58. *This view shows the alterations made by the U.D.C. in 1926, to provide a council chamber and other rooms on the first floor.*

59.   A view of the Civic Centre, officially opened by the Duchess of Kent on 8 December 1983.

the same time selling to him the land at Burton Farm. Unfortunately the land at Bybrook was let to John Hobbs on a long lease that did not expire until 1919, and he refused to vacate earlier. The Local Government Board refused to approve a compulsory purchase order so, to meet the immediate needs, the Council bought from Burra over one acre of land adjoining the old cemetery in Canterbury Road. The old burial ground in Station Road was made into a public garden in 1931.

Even before the agreement with London, the Council had provided much additional housing. Between the wars estates in south Ashford were developed, and in the town centre houses were built in Norwood Gardens, largely to replace those demolished in slum clearance schemes. The area of Gravel Walk (to the south of New Street) had been notorious in the 19th century as a haunt of petty criminals and prostitution, and the poor housing was cleared under an Order approved by the Minister in 1934. In total 741 houses were built during the inter-war years.

Immediately after the war 144 pre-fabricated houses were erected to meet urgent needs, and by 1960 about 1,500 permanent houses were built by the Council, the majority in south Ashford, but with substantial numbers in Kennington and Willesborough.

Another major development in the 1970s was the building of the Stour Centre. This multi-purpose sports centre was erected on land between the two rivers, which had been bought in 1961. The first phase was opened in February 1975, and the second opened officially on 25 February 1978. Part of the same land was used for the erection of the new Civic Centre, officially opened by the Duchess of Kent on 8 December 1983. Against these additional functions, the Urban District lost trading undertakings in the post-war nationalisation programmes. The gas and electricity undertakings, and the isolation hospital were transferred to national boards in 1948.

60 & 61.   The County School for Girls was opened in 1907 in the house on the corner of Station Road and Dover Place, called Fairlawn. The picture below is of the girls playing croquet.

The County Council also saw its powers and duties alter considerably in this century. The first major change was made by the Education Act of 1902. This made the County Council responsible for schools in most of Kent (abolishing the Ashford School Board) and gave greater powers to develop higher education. The first higher school for girls was opened in Station Road, in a house on the corner of Dover Place called Fairlawn. The school was re-located in Maidstone Road in new buildings in 1927, and with extensions made in 1959 is today the Highworth school.

A new technical school was erected in Elwick Road in 1914 (used as a VAD hospital during the war) and in 1924 a school for girls was opened in the same building. New primary schools were built to meet the needs of the growing population—Bond Road (1946), Stanhope (1951), Beaver Green (1954) and others. Senior schools were established in Jemmett Road, south Ashford in 1931 (later Rothelawe School, closed in 1990), and in the old grammar school buildings in Hythe Road and in Essella Road (now the North School) in 1933. The new grammar school for boys, now the Norton Knatchbull School, was opened in 1958.

The County Council also had responsibility for main roads. In order to provide employment in the difficult 1920s, they introduced a plan to improve the main road between Maidstone and the coast—now the A20. Bypasses were planned in 1924 for all of the towns and villages on this route. The detailed planning of the Ashford bypass was started in 1929 but, for several reasons including the outbreak of war, this was not completed until July 1957. Until that time the growing volume of traffic had to pass through the town, with the difficult bends in Castle Street and the narrow and steep East Hill.

The County Council adopted the provisions of the Libraries Acts, and in 1928 provided the first public library in Ashford, in Station Road. This was said to be the first purpose built library building in Kent, but older readers will remember it as a wooden structure. With the growth of the town, the new library in Church Road (on a site of houses destroyed by bombing during the war), was opened in January 1965.

The old scheme for the relief of the poor by the Guardians was abolished by the Local Government Act of 1929, and the responsibility given to the County Council. This was not to be a long standing arrangement—some powers were transferred to the National Assistance Board in 1934, and the whole service nationalised by the National Assistance Act of 1948. Thus from the early 19th century the responsibility for this service had been transferred from the smallest unit of government (the parish) to the largest.

The volunteer fire brigade was absorbed into the the National Fire Service from 14 April 1942. The need for a public service covering the whole of the country was thought necessary after the war, and the County Council was given this responsibility.

Transport Although improved locomotives and services were provided by the railway company, no major changes occurred until 1961. From 12 June the main line from London to Folkestone was electrified, together with those to Maidstone and Canterbury (but not that to Hastings). The result was faster trains and a much improved and frequent service. At the same time the Ashford railway station and the bridge carrying the road to south Ashford were rebuilt. The international station now being built for passengers to board trains for mainland Europe, via the Channel Tunnel, will destroy all traces of the original station.

With road transport, the big change was, of course, the replacement of horse drawn vehicles by motor. The registration of motor cars was not required until the end of 1903, so that the details of their first appearance in the town is difficult to determine. The first

62. The date when the first motor car was seen in Ashford is not known, but was in the very first years of this century. Compulsory registration was not introduced until 1904, when Dr. Vernon registered two cars that had been owned by him for several years. One was a Benz Ideal, illustrated here.

63. Another early owner was Charles Hayward, who manufactured cycles and later had a garage business in New Street. This photograph, taken about 1919, shows his son (also Charles) and his wife driving this car, a 12 hp Darraque, in Chart Road.

two private cars registered both belonged to Dr. Claude Vernon, a medical practitioner and medical officer of health to the town. On 1 December 1903 he registered (as D21 and D22) an eight horse power Argyle voiturette and a three h.p. Benz Ideal car. These vehicles were probably not new, since the Benz was available from 1899 and the Argyle from 1902, and the *Kentish Express* for 13 October 1900 reported that Dr. Vernon had used his car to go to vote in the general election. To the end of 1905 only 15 cars were registered in Kent to Ashford residents, which included D1333 for a Darracq by Charles Hayward, a garage proprietor in New Street. The same registration was used for many years on different vehicles by his son and grandson.

With public transport details are also scarce. The first reference to a motor bus is 1909, when a service to Kennington was started by Henry Thomas Dew. No vehicle was, however, registered in his name, so he probably used a second-hand bus. This service continued until about 1919. Dew had bought a new Commer bus in 1913, so the service was obviously successful.

The regular routes to neighbouring towns did not start until some years after 1909, by which time both the East Kent and the Maidstone and District Companies were operating. As an example, the route to Faversham by the Maidstone & District company started on 21 August 1915.

Health Services   The Cottage Hospital in Wellesley Road continued in use until after the first war. It was then considered that a new and larger hospital was necessary to provide the best treatment. The old hospital was governed by a board appointed under a scheme approved by the Charity Commissioners, and they set about the task of raising enough money from voluntary sources to achieve this. By 1926 they had raised sufficient to start, and on 20 October the Duke and Duchess of York (afterwards King George VI and Queen

Elizabeth) laid the foundation stone of a new hospital in King's Avenue. The hospital was opened on 1 July 1928. Fund raising continued, and on 6 November 1930 a nurses' hostel was opened by Princess Helen Victoria. In 1935 a night nurses' hostel was built. This hospital was taken over by the National Health Service on 6 July 1948. The new district hospital at Willesborough, the William Harvey, was opened in April 1979.

The Ashford St John's Ambulance Brigade continued to give good service. A horse drawn ambulance was bought in 1907, replaced by the first motor ambulance in 1921. The regular ambulance service was provided by the health service from 1948, but the St John's brigade continues to give invaluable service in training and providing additional voluntary cover for special events. Their hall in Maidstone Road, named after Sir John Furley, was opened in 1966.

Wartime   Many attempts were made in the 19th century to find a way of making manned flights. Considerable success was achieved with lighter-than-air machines, but the direction of flight was determined solely by the prevailing winds. This was clearly demonstrated in Ashford on 2 November 1880 when Henry Coxwell, a well-known and experienced aviator, brought his balloon to the town. This was filled with town gas and Coxwell, with two companions, set off hoping to make a cross-channel flight. The wind was blowing strongly from the east, so instead of the intended direction the balloon was carried westward, and after a flight of nine and a half hours they landed safely in Devonshire, having at one stage of the journey reached a height of 8,000 feet.

64.   *Wright type A aeroplane belonging to Alec Ogilvie at Camber, Sussex, c.1911. This was the first type of aeroplane to be built in any number, not only in the U.S.A. but under licence in France and in this country by Short's. The achievements of this machine include the first flight by a European to last more than one hour (in 1909), and the first non-stop double crossing of the Channel (in 1910). A crash whilst flying a modified version caused the death of Hon. C.S. Rolls (of Rolls-Royce) in 1912.*

The first flight by a power-driven heavier-than-air aeroplane was made by Orville Wright in America in 1903. Development continued thereafter in a number of countries, and in 1908 the two Wright brothers demonstrated their plane in France. These trials were observed by an English army officer who remarked, 'that Wilbur Wright is in possession of a power which controls the fate of nations is beyond dispute'. It is unlikely that those Ashfordians who went to Barrow Hill on the morning of 22 May 1911 to see the first aeroplane ever seen in the town can have visualised the changes that this new invention would bring. The plane was piloted by Alec Ogilvie, who was making a journey from Camber, near Rye, to his new home at Eastchurch on the Isle of Sheppey. He followed the railway line from Rye, but found it necessary to land in Mr. Pledges's field at Barrowhill (about where the Highworth school is now) to replenish his water supply. He afterwards took off, and completed his flight successfully.

The new possibilities for air travel were many years in the future, but their use in war was not so long delayed. Troops were stationed in Ashford during the first war, but otherwise the impact was limited to the losses of those who joined the armed forces, and to the limited air raids. The first of these was on 15 August 1915, when a zeppelin airship dropped both incendiary and explosive bombs on Queen's Road and the Warren. A daylight raid by aircraft was made in 1917, which resulted in the death of one person in south Ashford.

65.   The dedication ceremony at the war memorial in Church Road, on 1 June 1924.

After the war land in Church Road, for many centuries part of the vicarage glebe land, was acquired by trustees, and a war memorial was erected. This was unveiled by General Sir Ian Hamilton on 1 June 1924, and the gardens adjoining opened in 1927.

At the beginning of the Second World War Ashford was a reception area, receiving evacuees from London to what was then thought to be a safe area. This changed completely with the fall of France in May 1940. Although much of the Battle of Britain was fought in the skies of Kent, air raid damage was surprisingly light. The railway works, then involved in war production, were an obvious target. The possibility of invasion was a real threat, and taken very seriously, although in 1940 these preparations were largely improvised. After the middle of September the Germans abandoned any immediate plans for invasion but, despite this, the threat remained and, following a visit by (then) Lieut. Gen. Montgomery in May 1941, it was decided to make Ashford a strongly defended and tank-proof town. Explosives were placed in pipes that ran for over one mile and the outer wire obstacle was more than four miles long. The intention was that, if invasion occurred, there would be no withdrawal under any circumstances, and Ashford would hold out to the last against all attacks. Despite all these preparations, many civilians continued to live in the town, and most were unaware of the extent of the plans for defending the town. Plans were made for civilians to be evacuated immediately if an invasion started. By the summer of 1942 this threat had virtually disappeared, and the plans had never to be implemented.

Air raids, however, continued. In all there were 2,869 air raid alerts and 118 incidents. Eighty-three persons were killed and 321 injured, while 138 houses were destroyed and 8,478 damaged.

Entertainments and Sports   Spectator entertainments and sports on the scale that they are known today were largely unknown until the present century. Cricket was played from a very early date in Kent, and Ashford is known to have had an away match against Wye in 1743—the year before the first national rules were agreed in London. A field near Chart Leacon is called the 'Cricketing field' in a deed of 1797, and at this time Edward Hussey, who lived in Ashford as a young man (his father, Thomas, had a house in North Street), played for Kent and England. In 1847 cricket is said to have been played on a pitch south of the churchyard, and by 1851 on land at Barrow Hill, defined by one writer as the present pitch. Cricket was certainly played here in 1888, but this was stopped by William Pledge, tenant of Barrowhill Farm, because of the nuisance. It may be that this was more casual play and not the town team, since the obituary of Richard James in 1905 states that he was a regular player for the town team 40 years earlier on a pitch where Kent and Sussex Avenues now stand. The area at the top of New Street was known as Barrow Hill at that time, and it therefore seems likely that this was the location of the town pitch. When this area was developed about 1880, a new pitch was found at the end of Dover Place, and after about ten years another move was made to a pitch south of Godinton Road. After the break caused by the First World War, the club was revived and the first match was played on the present ground at Barrowhill on 11 May 1921.

Indoor stage entertainment was a rare event. The Ashford vestry was firmly oppose to stage performances, and the rules they adopted in 1786 include a determination to support the magistrates to prevent players from performing a play in the town more than once in 10 years! A company of actors led by Mr. Perry was advertised in 1750, and early in the next century there is a reference to a theatre in Castle Street. This is most likely to have been in an outbuilding in the yard of the *Castle* inn.

66 & 67.   *Two photographs of outings—the cause is unknown, but all are men! The first with a horse-drawn conveyance is assembled outside the* Wellesley *hotel at the beginning of this century. The second, taken a few years later outside the* British Volunteer *in New Street. The charabanc was first registered by Ernest Wills of Cheriton in May 1913.*

68.   The Corn Exchange decorated for the Coronation exhibition of 1911.

69.   The Coronation day parade, 1911.

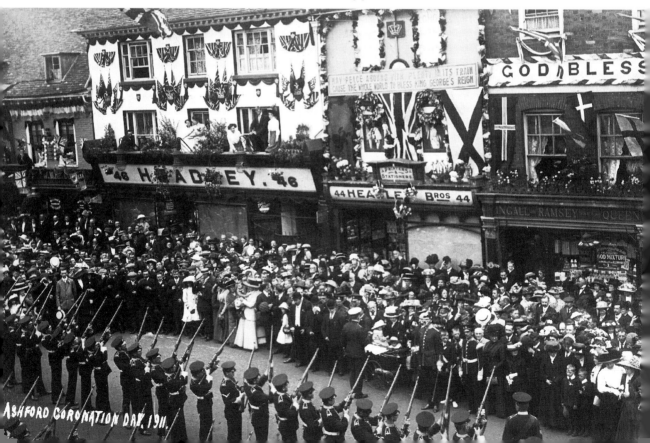

Assemblies for dancing and cards were advertised in the mid-18th century at the *Saracen's Head* during the winter, to take place on the Thursdays after the full moon—more convenient in the absence of any street lighting. Reference has already been made to the reconstruction of the old court house to provide new assembly rooms during the period of the Napoleonic war. The demand for these had disappeared by 1840, when it was stated that no assembly had taken place for three successive years.

In Victorian Ashford concerts were held in the public rooms (the old assembly rooms). As an example, the first issue of the *Ashford and Alfred News* (the forerunner to the *Kentish Express*) advertised two grand concerts by Kalozdy's Hungarian Band.

A form of entertainment that was a great attraction to the population of Victorian England was the grand exhibition. Nationally, of course, the greatest of these was that held in the Crystal Palace in Hyde Park, London in 1851, but later in the century (and afterwards) several were held in Ashford. In 1894 the exhibition, held in the Corn Exchange and the market buildings, was the scene of a grand display. The exhibition was opened by the Princess Christian (Helena, wife of Prince Christian of Schleswig-Holstein), described by the report in the *Kentish Express* as the most gracious of the Queen's daughters. She arrived by special train punctual to the minute, to be met by the Lord Lieutenant as well as the local dignitaries, and the chairman of the railway company. There were several such exhibitions in following years and they included not only trade stands by local as well as national companies, but also displays of articles lent by local people and examples of their handicraft. Another such exhibition was held (at the same time as a cricket week) in 1911 to mark the coronation of King George V.

The present century saw the introduction of the moving picture, an invention which captured the public interest to an extent not previously achieved by any single form of entertainment. It provided an alternative to public houses for adults, and an ideal way of keeping children off of the streets and from under their mothers' feet. At first the performances were provided by travelling equipment, the show taking place in any convenient hall. An example is the show given by Mr. Gerald Hunt in the Corn Exchange in September 1906, which included caricatures of Ashford celebrities as well as pictures of a royal wedding in Spain and life in Russia. Within a few years permanent cinemas were being provided, the first in Ashford being the Palace in Tufton Street. It was described as palatial in appearance, comfortable and large inside and fitted up in the most luxurious manner. Unfortunately, the opening performance on 18 December 1911 was spoilt by the failure of the lighting system—the electricity had to be generated in the building since a public supply was not to come for another 15 years. Prices ranged from 3d. to 1s. 0d. for the balcony which had green velvet seats and a red carpet.

The Royal cinema in Beaver Road (just south of the railway station) first opened in June 1912, and the Odeon in the High Street on 31 August 1936. Post-war changes, with the introduction of television and other forms of home entertainment, have reduced the demand for the cinema and now the last, the Royal (known in later years simply as the Cinema) has been demolished to allow the building of new roads.

In the inter-war years theatrical performances were given in the Corn Exchange, but in 1925 the County theatre in Station Road, later part of the Ashford Working Men's club, was opened.

Football had its supporters with many small teams formed from members of schools or clubs. The first town team was formed about 1880, and associated with the railway employees, and called the South Eastern Rangers. At about the same time a team called the Kentish Express was formed, although not all of the players were employed by the newspaper. In

70.   *Ashford's first cinema, the Picture Palace in Tufton Street. The building is now a furniture store.*

71.   *The Royal cinema in Beaver Road before the last war. This was the last cinema in Ashford to be closed, but has now been demolished to make way for the new international railway station.*

72.   The Bowls Club, at the corner of Vicarage and Church Roads.

1891 these two clubs amalgamated to form Ashford United, playing on a ground at the rear of the *Victoria* inn in Beaver Road. A few years later the club moved to a pitch south of Godinton Road. This was the first enclosed pitch used by the club, and there were several successes in Kent cup matches. Despite this, however, the club did not receive sufficient support, and the heavy debts resulted in cessation in 1907. A new club was formed, called the Ashford Railway Works, which played on a ground off Newtown Road from 1908 until 1928. After a break of two years, a new club was formed, which acquired the ground off Essella Road in 1930.

Golf was first played on a small course in Godinton Park, opened with seven holes in 1904. By the following year another two holes and a club house had been added. A few years later the club leased 41 acres at Bybrook, on land belonging to the Burra estate, although the club was a sub-tenant of John Hobbs. After the war this land was sold for development, so the club moved to a new golf course on 130 acres of land in Sandyhurst Lane. Ten acres, the frontage land, was sold for development. During the war the land was used by troops, except for about twenty acres which was fenced off for agriculture. This part was not returned to the club after the war, and in 1950 a new course was laid out by a golf architect. This is the course used today, subject to the changes made as a result of the recent building of the M20 motorway.

The Bowls club on the corner of Vicarage Lane and Church Road first opened on 12 May 1909.

Conclusion   The building of the Channel tunnel and an international passenger station in Ashford is bringing many major changes. New industrial and commercial activities are planned, with a further substantial increase in population. Ashford seems certain to enter the 21st century as a major centre, not only as in the past for East Kent, but important in a much wider sphere.

Appendix I
Extract from Domesday Book

In Lest de Wiwarlet.   *In Langebrige Hind.*

Iſtē Maigno ten̄ de Hugone *Estefort* . Turgiſus tenuit de Goduino
7 ꝓ uno ſolin ſe deſd . Tṛa . ē dimid car̄ . In dn̄io tam̄ . ē una car̄ . 7 ii .
uilli hn̄t . i . car̄ . Ibi . ii . ſerui . 7 viii . ac̄ ṗti .

T.R.E. ualeb̄ . xxv . ſolid . Q̇do recep̄ : xx . ſol . Modo : xxx . ſolid .

Ipſe Hugo ten̄ *Essella* . Tres hōēs tenuer̄ de rege . E . 7 potuer̄ ire
quoliḃ cū tris ſuis . ꝓ . iii . jugis ſe deſd . Tṛa . ē . i . car̄ 7 dimid .
Ibi m̄ . iiii : uilli cū . ii . bord hn̄t . i . car̄ . 7 vi . ac̄s ṗti .

Totū T.R.E. ualeb̄ . xx . ſolid . 7 poſt : xv . ſolid . Modo : xx . ſolid .

Aliā *Essetesford* ten̄ Maigno de hugone . Wirelm tenuit
de rege . E . ꝓ uno ſolin ſe deſd . Tṛa . ē . iiii . car̄ . In dn̄io ſuȳ . ii .
7 ii . uilli cū . xv . bord hn̄t . iii . car̄ . Ibi æccła 7 pbr̄ . 7 iii . ſerui .
7 ii . molin̄ de x . ſolid 7 ii . den .

T.R.E. ualeb̄ . lxx . ſol . 7 poſt : lx . ſol . Modo : c . ſol .

         In Cert hd̄.

Ipſe abb̄ ten̄ uñ jugū *Rapentone* . 7 Anſered de eo .
7 ꝓ uno jugo ſe deſd . Tṛa . ē . ii . car̄ . In dn̄io . ē una . cū . iiii .
bord . Ibi . xi . ac̄ ṗti . 7 q̇rta pars molini de . xv . den . 7 ſilua
. x . porc̄ . 7 adhuc h̄r̄ . ii . juga quæ de ſuo dn̄io dedit ei abb̄ .
7 ibi . ii . uilloſ cū . viii . bord . T.R.E. 7 poſt : ualuit . iii . lib .

               £ Modo . iiii . lib .

In the Lathe of WYE
In LONGBRIDGE Hundred

Maino also holds (South) ASHFORD from Hugh. Thorgils held it
from Earl Godwin. It answers for 1 sulung. Land for ½ plough.
In lordship, however, 1 plough.
  2 villagers have 1 plough.
  2 slaves; meadow, 8 acres.
Value before 1066, 25s; when acquired 20s; now 30s.

Hugh holds ESSELLA himself. Three men held it from King Edward;
they could go wherever [they would] with their lands. It answers
for 3 yokes. Land for 1½ ploughs.
  Now 4 villagers with 2 smallholders have 1 plough.
  Meadow, 6 acres.
Value of the whole before 1066, 20s; later 15s; now 20s.

Maino holds the other ASHFORD from Hugh. Wirelm held it from
King Edward. It answers for 1 sulung. Land for 4 ploughs.
In lordship 2.
  2 villagers with 15 smallholders have 3 ploughs.
  A church and a priest, 3 slaves; 2 mills at 10s 2d.
Value before 1066, 70s; later 60s; now 100s.

In CHART Hundred
  The Abbot holds 1 yoke (in) RIPTON himself and Ansered from
  him. It answers for 1 yoke. Land for 2 ploughs. In lordship 1, with
    4 smallholders.
    Meadow, 11 acres. ¼ mill at 15d; woodland, 10 pigs.
  Further, he has 2 yokes which the Abbot gave him from his lordship
  and
    2 villagers with 8 smallholders.
  Value before 1066 and later £3; now £4.

Appendix II
Owners of Ashford Manor

1086 Maigno holds of Hugo de Montfort in Domesday Book

c.1100 Robert de Montfort, grandson of Hugo

c.1120 Norman de Ashford

c.1250 William de Ashford

c.1267 Simon de Criol and wife Maud, daughter of William de Ashford

1270 Roger de Leybourne, by purchase from Maud and her second husband Roger de Rollyng

1271 William de Leybourne, son of Roger

1309 Juliana of Leybourne, granddaughter of William

1362 to King for charitable purposes, by grant of Juliana

1382 Dean & Canons of the Chapel of St Stephen, Westminster, by grant by the King. In 1384 the manor was granted to Sir Simon de Burley, but returned to the Dean & Canons in 1388.

1538 to King, on dissolution of the Chapel

1549 Sir Anthony Aucher of Otterden, by purchase

1556 Sir Andrew Judde of London, on foreclosure of mortgage

1558 Thomas Smythe and wife Alice, daughter and heir of Andrew Judde

1591 Sir John Smythe, son of Thomas

1608 Sir Thomas Smythe (Viscount Strangford from 1628), son of John

1635 Philip, 2nd Viscount Strangford, son of Thomas

1708 Henry Roper, 8th Lord Teynham, and wife Catherine (died 1711), daughter of Philip

1718 Lord Teynham married Ann, dau of Thomas Lennard, Earl of Sussex

1723 Ann, Lady Teynham on death of Henry

1725 Hon Robert Moore and Ann, Lady Teynham married

1755 Trevor and Charles Roper, grandsons of Henry and Catherine Roper, infants and co-heirs in gavelkind

1765 Rev. Francis Hender Foote of Bishopsbourne, by purchase after Act of Parliament, 29 Geo II, c.24 (1756)

1773 Mrs. Catherine Foote, widow of Francis

1776 John Foote, son of Francis and Catherine

1804 Robert Foote, son of John

1805 George Elwick Jemmett, by purchase (trustee Thomas Dawes, brother in law of George Elwick Jemmett)

1831 George Elwick Jemmett II, son of GEJ I (trustee until 1840 William Jemmett, brother of GEJ I)

1871 George Elwick Jemmett III and William Francis Bond Jemmett sons of GEJ II

1904 George Elwick Jemmett III on division of estates

1923 George Elwick Jemmett III died, leaving three daughters (his only son George Elwick Jemmett IV having been killed in the war). Maud, the last daughter died, unmarried, in 1951.

Manor Stewards or bailiffs

	Steward	Deputy[1]
1516	Sir Edward Poyninge	John Hall
by 1559	William Padnall	
1584	Henry Quested	
1585	Nicholas Gurney	
1592	Ralph Quested	
1599	Edward Hall	
1608	John Hawtry, buried 1638[2]	
1638	John Nevill, buried 1641[2]	
c.1640	Richard Martin	
1651	Henry Viall	
?	Robert Mellowe buried 1656[2]	
c.1668	Henry Bennett	
1671	Richard May	
1700	George Sinnott	
1752	Henry Franklin	Josias Pattenson
1771	Josias Pattenson	Samuel Munn
1779	Samuel Munn	George Jemmett
1795	George Jemmett	George Elwick Jemmett
1804	George E. Jemmett[3]	James Tappenden
1831	Edwin Beresford Dawes	(1834) John James Bond
1835	William Cruttenden	
1845	Charles Mercer	
1855	Robert Furley	(1861) Frederick Hughes Hallett
1868	Frederick Hughes Hallett	
1901	James Turner Welldon	

[1] in addition deputy stewards were appointed for specific cases, particularly where the parties lived away from Ashford. The transaction would be dealt with 'out of Court' before that deputy steward, and enrolled as such subsequently.

[2] described in burial register as bayliffe or bayley.

[3] also Lord of Manor, but that position exercised by trustee.

Appendix III

Ashford Custumal or Customary Booke

Contayninge the lawes and customes of the tennantes copyholders of the Deane & Canons of the kinges free Chaple of our blessed Ladye virgine, & St Stephen the first martyr within the kinges Pallaice at Westminster of their manners of Eshetesford and Esture in Kent: To the which the Tennantes and Copyholders of the same Manners have assented and agreed in manner & forme as in Articles hereafter following playnlye is declared & expressed All which Customes and Articles at the Court houlden in Eshetesford aforesayd the third daye of October in the yeare of our lord god 1516; & the eight yeare of the Raygne of Kinge Henery the eight in the presence of Sir Edward Poyninge Knight Chiefe Steward of the Courtes of the sayd Deane & Canons in the Countye of Kent & Richard Rawson Cannon Stewarde and visitor of the said Colledg John Halles Learned man understewarde of the sayd Courte & in the presence of the Tennantes in the full Court the Articles aforesayd were openly red Afore the tennantes of Landes & tenements at the will of the Lorde to the which articles & Customes they gave their consentes etc

1   FIRST that every tennante that shall take any Landes by copy shall take the same openly in the Court to paye yearly such Rents as of old tyme hath bene payed due for the same upon copies sufficiently made therof & that the landes be expressed certeinlye in the Court Rolle & copies therof as by acres Rodds half acres yeards and boundes & meetes of the same.

2   ITEM that the copyes bee taken of the sayd Deane & Cannons according to the name of there corporacion that is to saye by the name Afore expressed, etc.

3   ITEM yf any copyholder have his copye not according to the sayd name of corporacion then he shall renew it after the sayd forme & to take it according to the sayd name Athis syde the feast of Easter which shalbe in the yeare of our Lord god 1517 upon payne of forfayture therof & for such renewing of there copyes after the sayd Corporacon pay no fine but to have it as they had it before.

4   ITEM that everye Copyeholder at his entre be it by decent purchase exchange or performanse of will from henceforth make & paye to fine as much money as the half yearely Rent of the whole Copyhold shall be by one yeare and none otherwise. PROVIDED also that the sayd Article of fines of the half yearely Rent at the entre not extend the shoppes now buylded in the market place for market folkes as buchers & such other market folkes for there first entre which every of the takers by Copie shall make & have after the date hereof and after to paye such fine as other Copyholders shall doe like as aforesayd.

5   ITEM yf that any ground be taken to be buylded within the sayd market place by any of the tennants which shall take the same for the intent to buyld uppon the same & in consideracion therof there to be the lesse Rents Reserved according as it was in value at the tyme of the coppie made which land so buylded is after to amore yearely value by reason of the sayd buylding & amendment all fines to be made by an other person or persons for their entre in the same uppon any new coppies made shalbe according to the value of the landes buylded as it is at the tyme of the sayd copye new to be taken & not onlye according to the value before the buyldinge etc

6   ITEM that no man hold neither occuppie any Landes or tenements parcells of this manner unlesse there be made therof a sufficient entre in the Court Rolle and also the person to have of the same accopye of that Court Rolle in his owne possession under payne of forfayture of his Coppyholde etc

7   ITEM that no Coppyholder do wast ne ffell no Okes, Elmes neither other great woodes or Tymber meete for Tymber buylding neither younge Okes Elmes or other woode like to grow to be tymber but the sayd great Woodes & kinde of the same with all hedgerowes and named woodes called Hempsted woode, Virtwoode & Southwoode & all other named woodes of the sayd manner & lordship or within any Landes or tenements of the same Deane & Cannons & all Tymber to be reserved to the lord upon payne of forfayture the copyholds & that the lord may lawfuly fell & Carry away the sayd Okes Elmes & all the sayd great woode & Tymber & kinde therof at there pleasure.

8   ITEM that the Lords shall have for them & their Tennant Copyholders wayes necessarie over the landes taken by Copye though no mencion therof be made in the coppye etc

9   ITEM that every Copyholder that hath any Copyhouses or other buyldings upon there Copyholdes shall sufficiently uphold keep maynteine & repaire the same houses & buyldings upon payne of forfayture of all there Coppyholdes & lands holden by Copy if it be not reformed within half ayeare after dew monicion given by the steward or officer for tyme being of the sayd manner to any tennante so defaltinge or beinge negligent.

10   ITEM that all tennantes having tenement or tenements by Copye now buylded or hereafter to bee buylded haveing landes of Copyhold shall not alyen any of there copylandes from their sayd tenement or tenements of Copyholds neither there tenements from there Copyhold landes upon payne of forfayture of his sayd whole Copyhold etc

11   ITEM that every Copyholder that will bargaine sell Alyen or declare his will or to make lease for any tyme above one yeare of any Copyhold landes or tenements shall make theof Surrender openly in the Court to the entent of that bargaine sale Aliencion lease or to the entent to make his will or else out of Court before the baylife or his deputy or two other tennantes at the least freeholders or coppyholders of the same manner upon payne of forfayture of there copyholdes so bargayned sold Alyened or letten contrarye to the sayd ordinance & that all wills & Testaments therof made without such surrender had shalbe voyd & had for nought & that all such Surrender out of Court so had shalbe presented witnessed & testified by the sayd Baylife or his Deputy and by the sayd tennants or two of them at next or second Court to be holden at that mannor or els the sayd Surrender so made out Court to be voyd etc

12   ITEM yf any tennant dye seased of Copyhold having two sonnes or more then the eldest sonn shall have the same Copyhold paying to his other brother or brethren after the rate the value of theire portions within one year next after any of the same brothers shalbe of the age of one & twenty yeares & to find Suretye or otherwise to be provided by the Court for the same upon that condition at tyme of the taking of his copy & that value to by tryed by the tennantes copyholders apearing at the Court when the death shalbe presented of the Copyholder that so dyed seased

13   ITEM if any tennant of Copyhold dye & no Surrender of his copyhold in Court neither out of Court before his death or els that Surrender out of Court not presented & witnessed as is above sayd & the next heire or heires or other that clayme tytle or interest come not into the Court within half yeare after the death of his or there Ancestor whose heire he or they be or after whose death clayme or pretend there tytle to take the land & by coppy of the sayd Court according to the custom then the Copyhold shalbe seased to the Lordes handes & at three Court dayes after the half yeare passed & at the sayd seasure had & made proclamacion shalbe made within the sayd Court that he that Claymeth to be heire or to have other interest to the same landes according to the Custom to come into the Court to be admytted therof tennante according to the custome & els the same lands shalbe at the will of the lordes which proclamacion shalbe entred & enrowled in the same Court & if none come as heire and soe prove himself or by other tytle within ayeare next after the death of the tennante that then his landes shall remayne unto the lordes as if such Coppie had never therof byn made etc

14 ITEM that surrender as is before sayd to be had & recorded in the Rolles of the sayd Courtes maye be made to the use of performans of willes declaring therin none therof to be intayled to the use of terme of life & other condicions of payment & not payment in like manner as landes of Charterhold may be made by estate of wrighting Allways advised & provided that every man that hath cause to enter in Remaynder or upon acondicion shall take the landes in the Court & paye the half fine of the whole yeares Rent as is before sayd etc

15 ITEM that every wife shalbe endowed of half the Copyhold that her husband was of Estate of inheritance according to the Custome at any tyme in his life to have to her for terme of widdowhold provided & ordeined that the sayd Copyholder made nor commytted any forfayture of his copyhold in his life & provyded also that the sayd wife take her sayd dowrye of the lordes by anew coppie & paye fine as aforesayd.

16 ITEM that no lease of Copyholdes for terme of yeares be made above the terme of five yeares & that to be entred in the Courte Rolles & a copy therof to be had & if any be graunted above five yeares that graunt & licence to be voyd.

17 ITEM that no Copy be graunted to the use of any will not above to persons & dewring the life of the one & theye to paye the half fine etc

18 ITEM that no Copy be graunted in free ne tennante of life but to one person except it be to the husband & wife or for the entent to performe a last will of a copyholder or like as aforesayd & then to pay the whole fine.

19 ITEM that no Copyholder devide his Landes neither Apporcion the Rent of the same without the assent & licence of the Lordes or Steward of the Coledge or other there sufficient deputye obteyned under the writing or seale of the sayd Lordes & that to take by copye & to apeare in the Court Rolle under payne of forfayture.

20 ITEM that no Copyholder Alyen or sell under the quantitye of one acre of his land to no man & that after such sale or Alyenacion the Lordes Rent to be apporcioned out of the parcells of Landes which were before in one hand after the goodnes yearlye value of the parcells & not after the quantitye & in case where Copyholdes shall dissend to divers heires there shall never particion be made so that anye of the heires shall have under the quantity of one acre & then the Rent of the Lordes to be apporcioned after the goodnes of the land like as aforesayd etc

21 ITEM that no tennante or tennantes shall Alyen change or sell any Copyhold Landes without consent of the Deane & Channons or there sufficient deputye & to such one as they will admytt & at every such Alyenacion change or sale shall paye the half fine of there yearlye Rent unto the Lordes & if two Copyholders change there Copyelands one with another each of them to paye the half fine like as before expressed etc

22 ITEM that no tennant of Copyhold shall do make no manner of transmutacion of possession of there Copyholdes to be made Charterhold that is to saye by ffeffement Release Recoverye fine at the Comen Law or make any lease for terme of life or other mans life by deed or otherwise nor put no bill before the Chanceler of England the King's Justice or the King's Councell for to trye any matter of Custom or Conscience of any Landes holden by Coppie that then all such to be forfayted to the Lordes of the sayd manner for ever & also all other Copyland the which the sayd tennant or tennants hold or holdeth of the sayd manner to be forfayted to the sayd Lordes etc

23 ITEM all variances debates questions accions & sutes for & concerning any copyhold in the law shalbe tryed in the sayd Court by playnt in nature of his accion & so the issue joyned to be tryed by homage of Copyholders & if any copyholder be somoned to apeare to answer any such playnt affirmed & comes not he shall lose at the first tyme vi d at the second tyme xii d at the third tyme ii s & the fourth daye his copyhold to be seased & remayne in the hands of the Lordes unto the next Court & then if he come not the playntife or demandant

shall have Tenerye out of the Lordes hands by Copy according to his demand & his expences costes & damages sustained in the same.

24   ITEM all matters in Conscience of Copyhold to be sued by bill in the same Court & tryed by proses.

25   ITEM everye Copyholder to make his sute the next Court after St Michaell & Easter or to be amerced at every Court xii d & that no wright called 'bre de Aturnato faciendo' shall not be allowed nor excuse of the sayd amersmentes to Copyholders.

26   ITEM the Copyholders shall keepe defence & Closure of there Copyholds.

27   ITEM all Rents of Copyholders to be payd at the feastes of the anunciacion of our Ladye & St Michaell by even porcions or at the next Court holden after either of those feastes on payne of forfayture of there Copyholds.

28   ITEM that all Copyholders of those sayd Manners and dwellings within the Presinct of the sayd lordship shall grinde all the corne which they shall occupy in there houses or otherwise at or in the Lordes Mill of this sayd manner of Eshetisford except the sayd Mill stand for lak of repraciones or water or otherwise to be lett in default of the Lordes or miller upon payne of forfayture every tyme iiii d to the Lordes etc

29   ITEM the misdemener of Copyholders contrarye to the premises or anye of them to be cause of forfayture of there Copyhold or otherwise used or suffered to be used

30   ITEM that if any other & further question that maye happen or arise in the premises or any of them or any other Landes or tenementes of Copyhold of this sayd manner that now be or here after shalbe declared interpreted & put in certaine by the sayd Lordes of the sayd Colledge & there Learned Counsell & so to be entred as Custome incident to the Copyholdes into this Customarie.

31   ITEM that no Copyholder break or make any issue in or through the banke of the streame there running to the mill under payne of forfayture of his Copyhold & that they cast no nett or netts or by any grime or grimes well or wells or any hoockes or baytes within the sayd water wherby the Lordes royalte shold minysh or decaye under payne aforesayd etc 32 Item yf any tennant or tennants of Copyhold dwelling within the presinct of the sayd Lordship know or knowne any forfayture by any of the sayd tennantes to be made or breaking any of the sayd Articles afore expressed & doe not present it or doe it to be presented at the Court next Court daye after the sayd forfayture is made that then he shall forfayte his owne Copyhold & it to remayne in the Lordes hands to be disposed at theire pleasure.

from Centre for Kentish Studies, U1045 M 25

Appendix IV
Manor Court Baron

The Manor to wit The Court Baron

of

Ashford

of Edward Louisa Mann Esquire and Benjamin Hatley ffoote Esquire[1] Lords of the said Manor holden at the Courthouse in the Town of Ashford in the county of Kent on Wednesday the fourteenth day of April in the Thirteenth Year of the Reign of our Sovereign Lord George the Third by the Grace of God of Great Britain ffrance and Ireland King Defender of the ffaith And in the year of our Lord one Thousand seven Hundred and Seventy three before Josias Pattenson Gentleman Steward of the said Court.

The Homage to wit Thomas Cheesman   Sworn
Edward Barrett
Charles Baker
and
Joseph Virrill[2]   Sworn

To this Court comes Thomas Bonner of Ashford aforesaid Taylor one of the customary Tenants of this Manor and Margaret his Wife in their own proper Persons and in full and open Court in the Presence of the said Homage to wit the said Thomas Cheesman Edward Barrett Charles Baker and Joseph Virrill four customary Tenants of this Manor (the said Margaret being first solely and separately examined apart from her said husband as the Custom is and the Law requires)[3] and surrender into the Hands of the Lords of the said Manor by the Hands and Acceptance of the said Josias Pattenson Steward of the said Court **To** the Use and Behoof of Charles ffagg of Ashford aforesaid Surgeon his Heirs and Assigns **One** piece of Copyhold Land (with a Building thereon being now laid open to and made part of the Garden[4] belonging to the said Thomas Bonner situate lying and being in Ashford aforesaid within the Jurisdiction of the said Manor abutting to the common Gutter[5] there called the copyhold Gutter towards the North to a common Way there called Saint Johns lane towards the South to copyhold Lands of Mr John Waterman in right of Martha his wife[6] towards the West and to a copyhold piece of Land late of Ann Barrett and now of the said Thomas Bonner being the other part of the said Garden towards the East containing by Estimation from the East to the West by the North three and Twenty ffeet and from the West to the East by the South Eighteen ffeet and ten Inches and from the North to the South by the West seventy six ffeet and eight Inches and from the North to the South by the East Eighty six ffeet and eight Inches late in the Tenure or Occupation of Justinian Butcher or his Assigns and now or late in the Tenure or Occupation of the said Thomas Bonner or his Assigns **holden** of the Lords of the said Manor at the Will of the Lords by copy of the Court Roll according to the Custom of the said Manor by ffealty Suit of Court[7] and by the Yearly Rent of fourpence halfpenny at the ffeasts of the Annunciation of the blessed Virgin Mary and Saint Michael the Archangel by even and equal Portions half Yearly to be paid and other accustomed Services **And thereupon** the Lords of the said Manor by the said Josias Pattenson Steward of the said Court grant unto the said Charles ffagg seisen thereof by the Rod to him Delivered **Except** and always reserved unto the said Lords their heirs and Assigns all and singular those things which according to the Custom of the said Manor ought or have been accustomed to be reserved **To have and to hold** the said copyhold or customary piece of Land and Premises with the Appurtenances except before excepted unto the said Charles ffagg his Heirs and Assigns **To** the only proper Use and Behoof of the said Charles ffagg and of his Heirs and Assigns for ever **To be holden** of the Lords of the said Manor at the Will of the Lords by Copy of Court Roll according to the Custom of the said Manor by ffealty Suit of Court and by the Yearly Rent of fourpence halfpenny of lawful Money of Great Britain at the ffeasts aforesaid half Yearly to be paid and all other Services therefore first due and of right accustomed according to the Custom of the said Manor **And also** paying to the said Lords their Heirs and Assigns after the death of every Tenant dying thereof siezed as after every Alienation or Surrender thereof made or to be made in the Name of a ffine for every Entry into the Premises to be had a Moiety of the Yearly Rent aforesaid according to the Custom of the said Manor And the said Charles ffagg is admitted Tenant to the said copyhold Premises with the Appurtenances and hath Possession thereof by the Rod to him delivered does his ffealty and gives to the Lords for a ffine for such his Entry into the Premises had twopence farthing being a Moiety of the Yearly Rent aforesaid according to the Custom of the said Manor.

   And afterwards at this same Court comes the said Charles ffagg in his own proper Person and in full and open Court in the Prescence of the said Homage, to wit, the said Thomas Cheesman Edward Barrett Charles Baker and Joseph Virrill four customary Tenants of the said Manor surrenders into the Hands of the Lord of the said Manor by the Hands and Acceptance of the said Josias Pattenson Steward of the said Court all and singular the said copyhold Lands and Premises above mentioned with the Appurtanances **To** the Use and Behoof of such Person and Persons for such Use and Uses Estate and Estates as the said Charles Fagg by his Last Will and Testament in Writing shall nominate devise direct limit or appoint according to the Custom of the said Manor **Yielding** and paying therefore unto the Lords of the said Manor the said Yearly Rent of fourpence halfpenny at the ffeasts aforesaid by Equal Portions halfyearly to be paid according to the Custom of the said Manor and all other Services therefore first due and of right accustomed And the said Charles ffagg gives to the Lord for a ffine for this his Surrender twopence farthing being a Moiety of the Yearly Rent aforesaid according to the Custom of the said Manor.[8]

[1] The names given as Lords are those of the executors of Rev. Francis Hender Foote, who died in 1773.
[2] By the end of the 18th century new owners were becoming more careless in observing the requirements of the manor customs, and the homage was usually only two persons.
[3] When a married man was admitted as tenant, his wife became entitled to one half of the property as dower, if widowed. This examination served to ensure she was aware of any potential loss of rights.
[4] This land was at the back of the premises later 13-15 High Street.
[5] The gutter was a drainage channel which ran from the butchers shops in Middle Row, behind the premises fronting the lower High Street and eventually drained into the river. All the frontage to the High Street was freehold, the land south of the gutter as far as the vicarage land was copyhold.
[6] This land had belonged to Martha Simpson, and had vested in her husband John Waterman on their marriage.
[7] This is the acknowledgement by the new tenant to appear at Court when required to do homage to the Lord of the Manor. It ceased to be imposed after 1811.
[8] The surrender to the persons in the will of the new tenant became standard practice in the 18th century, but abandoned in the early nineteenth. By such a surrender complications were avoided after the death of the tenant, and changes in the successor did not require further surrenders. It still required a valid will specifically providing for the devising of the copyhold land, otherwise the tenant was treated as intestate in this respect. When this happened, the succession was in accordance with the law of gavelkind.

from Centre for Kentish Studies, U 1045 M 10

Appendix V
Church Ministers

Parish Church

Pearman states that ministers were rectors until 1374, and then vicars. The reason for this is unclear, as Simon de Criol owned the advowson.

1282	Robert de Derby	
1316	William de Lucy	
1320	Martin Erchebaud	
1351	John de Gestyngthorp	
1351	Henry de Sudyngton	
1355	Thomas de Merston	
1361	Simon de Gaynesburgh	
1361	Adam Coriat or de Warwick	
1368	William Wyndesore	
1374	Richard de Borden	
1379	Richard de Cotyngham	
1380	Soloman Russell	
1390	Thomas Gerard	
1420	Richard Bochyer	
1436	Robert Hedyngham	
1460	Thomas Wilmot DD Oxon	
1469	William Wylmott. This appointment was apparently a temporary one, as Thomas Wylmot is again vicar in 1476 and he is described as vicar in his will of 1493.	
1493	William Sutton DD Oxon	1440? – 1503
1501	Hugh Hope MA Oxon	? – 1509
1509	Edward Mongeham BCL Oxon	1480? – 1512
1512	John White DD	? – 1519
1519	Richard Parkhurst MA Oxon	1485? – 1558
1547	John Ponet or Poynet DD Cantab	1514 – 1556
1551	Robert Foster	
1553	Thomas Knell	
1565	John Fuller	? – 1571
1571	Thomas Pett	? – 1579
1579	George Kerslake	
1581	Joseph Minge or Mynge BA Cantab	1555? – 1584
1584	John Holland BA Cantab	1560? – 1594
1594	Thomas Poulter MA	? – 1602
1602	John Wallis MA Cantab	1567 – 1622
1622	Edmund Hayes MA Cantab	? – 1638
1638	John Maccuby MA	
1643	Joseph Boden BA Oxon	1606 – ?
1647	Nicholas Prigg BA Cantab	1620? – 1696
	[see also Congregational Church]	
1662	Richard Whitlock BA Oxon	1616 – 1666
1667	Thomas Risden MA Cantab	1610 – 1673
1673	Samuel Warren BA Oxon	1640? – 1721
1721	John Clough MA Cantab	1689 – 1764

1765	Charles Coldcall MA Cantab	1722	–	1793
1765	James Andrew DD Oxon	1719	–	1791
1774	James Bond MA	1759	–	1826
1826	Thomas Wood	?	–	1847
1847	John Price Alcock MA Cantab	1808	–	1891
1888	Peter Francis Tindall MA Cantab	1856	–	1931
1914	Lionel Payne Crawford MA			
1915	Thomas Karl Sopwith MA			
1924	Harry William Blackburne DSO MC MA			
1931	Ronald Sutherland Brook Sinclair MC MA			
1938	Harry Duncan Storer Bowen MA			
1955	Neville Maurice Sharp MA			
1972	Aubrey K.W. Wright BA BD AKC			
1982	John Wilfred Everett MA			

Congregational Church

1662	Nicholas Prigg [see above]
1676	Thomas James
?	? Davies
?	Cornelius Handcock
1729	Thomas Gellibrand
1778	Joseph Gellibrand
1783	Evan Davies
1784-1809	no resident minister
1810	John Brackstone
1818	Josephus Chapman
1821	Robert Kemp
1825	John Elliott Hadlow
1845	Samuel R. Gibbs
1849	John F. James
1853	Alfred Turner
1895	Israel Phibus Thimann
1911	George Herbert Russell
1919	William Arthur Samuel
1925	A.J. Newton-Turner
1928	John Renison
1930	Sydney E. Archbell
1939	Frederick J. Paul

73.   The Congregational church on the opposite corner to the bowling green, on the site now occupied by the Magistrates' Courts. This church was built in 1866, replacing an older chapel that was built in 1820.

1942	David T. Scotland
1948	Ernest W. Southey
1952	Ernest S. Box

Baptist Church

1706	George Ellis	1827	James Payne
1727	John Ilden	1837	Thomas Davis
1733	George Green	1843	Henry Smith
1763	Samuel Brooks	1845	Thomas Clark
1772	James Brown appointed, but did not take office	1852	George H. Whitbread
1777	Benjamin Morgan	1859	Thomas Clark
1784	Thomas Cromwell	1874	Ebenezer Roberts
1794	Francis Read	1887	John Whitaker
?	James White	1906	William Lawrence Tweedie
1810	William Broady	1910	Walter Ridley Chesterton
1824	James Jackson	1920	James S.A. Warboys
		1922	Walter Archibald Weeks

Appendix VI

Market Charters and Grants

Charter to Simon de Criol, 13 October 1243

The King to the Archbishops [etc]
Know ye that we have granted and by this our charter have confirmed for us and our heirs to Simon de Criol and Maud, his wife, that they and their heirs for ever have free warren in all their demesne lands of Ashetesford, so that none shall enter those lands to chase in them or to take anything which to the said warren appertains without the licence and will of the said Simon and Maud and their heirs on our forfeiture of £10. And that they have at the same manor of Ashetesford one market every week on Saturday and one fair every year lasting for three days, to wit in the vigil and the day and the morrow of the Beheading of St John the Baptist unless that market and fair be to the damage [etc,etc]

Grant to William de Clynton, 7 April 1348

The King to William de Clynton, greeting. Know ye that we of our special grace, have granted and by this our charter confirm to our beloved subject William de Clynton, Earl of Huntington and Juliana, his wife, that they and the heirs of Juliana for ever have one fair every year at their manor of Eshetesford for three days duration, to wit, in the vigil, the day and in the morrow of St Anne so that such fair be not to the damage of neighbouring fairs. Wherefore we will and firmly order for us that the aforesaid Earl and Juliana and the heirs of Juliana for ever have the said fair at their aforesaid manor with all the liberties and free custom to such appertaining [etc,etc]

Grant to Dean and Canons of the Chapel of St Stephen, Westminster, 3 January 1466

Know ye that of our especial grace and from our certain knowledge we have granted and by this our charter confirm for us and our heirs to our beloved in Christ, the Dean and Canons of the College or Free Chapel of St Stephen within our Palace of Westminster and their successors, that they and their successors for ever have one fair at the vill of Eshetesford in the county of Kent every year for four days duration, to wit in the vigil and in the day of St John before the Latin Gate, and for two days next following, with all the liberties and free customs to such fair appertaining or belonging, unless such fair be to the damage of neighbouring fairs. Wherefore we will and firmly order for us and our heirs ... in the same manner, wholly, freely and quietly as any other fair formerly had or received of our gift, without disturbance, molestation, peturbation or impediment whatsoever. We grant also for us and our heirs to the aforesaid Dean and Canons and their successors that they for ever have and hold and also may have and hold all and all kinds of pleas of all and singular trespasses and contracts and other things and matters whatsoever at the time of the aforesaid fair in any way there emerging of all and singular flocking to the said fair or being there, to be held there in thew Court of the said Dean and Canons and their successors before their steward for the time being, and that all and singular to the said fair flocking and all others being there, coming there, staying and thence returning be free and quit of all kinds of arrests and perturbations of Justices, Escheators, Sheriffs, Stewards, coroners and clerks of the market of us, our heirs and successors aforesaid or their bailiffs or ministers whosoever, as well of and in their bodies as of and in their goods and chattels bringing and carrying or from the same taking and carrying away. And we grant to the aforesaid Dean and Canons and their successors for us and our heirs that they for ever have a certain Steward to be assigned at their will by the Dean and Canons and Steward to hold their Court of the aforesaid fair from time to time, so that express mention of the true yearly value of the premises or of or of other gifts and grants by us to the aforesaid Dean and

Canons and Steward before us made in these presents being less made or any statute, act or ordinance to the contrary made notwithstanding.

Grant to Philip, Viscount Strangford

We command you that by the oath of good and lawful men of your county, by whom the truth of the matter may be better known, you diligently enquire whether or not it be to the harm or prejudice of Us or of others, or to the hurt of any neighbouring market if We grant to Philip, Viscount Strangford, Lord of the Manor of Ashford in your County, and to his heirs that he, and his heirs and assigns may have and hold a market on every second Tuesday through the year within or next the town of Ashford in your County for ever, to be holden for buying and selling of all and all manner of beasts or cattle, goods and merchandise and to take the tolls and profits used in the said market to him and his heirs. And if it be to the harm or prejudice of Us, or of others, or to the hurt of any neighbouring market then to what harm and what prejudice of Us or of others, and to what hurt of any neighbouring market, and to whom and how and in what manner. And do you without delay send the requisition thereof distinctly and openly made to Us at Our Chancery Court under your seal and the seals of those by whom it shall have been made.

Witness Ourself at Westminster, 2nd June in 23rd year of Our Reign.[1671]

Inquisition taken at Ashford, 4th August in 23rd year of reign of Charles II

before me, William Hugesson, Kt., sheriff, by virtue of writ addressed to me and annexed to this requisition, by the oath of Nicholas Toke the younger, Richard Knevett, Walter Roberts, John Toke, George Moore, Edward Woodward, James Bate, Humphrey Wightwick, John Sturton, Daniel Nower, Robert Stace and Thomas Boys, good and lawful men of the county, who being there and sworn, and charged to enquire for the said Lord the King according to the exigency of the same writ say upon their oath THAT it is not to the harm and prejudice of the said King, nor of others, nor to the hurt of any neighbouring market if the King do grant that Philip, Viscount Strangford, may have and hold a market upon the every second Tuesday through the year within or next the town of Ashford.Grant to Philip, Viscount Strangford of a market every other Tuesday at Ashford.

8th November 1671

Appendix VII

Register Entries 1570–1839

	Marriages	Baptisms	Burials	Diff
1570 – 79	74	249	153	96
1580 – 89	89	375	298	77
1590 – 99	114	391	370	21
1600 – 09	91	422	297	125
1610 – 19	107	374	410	-36
1620 – 29	105	547	469	78
1630 – 39	75	460	372	88
1640 – 49	31[1]	244[1]	179[1]	65
1650 – 59	83[1]	287[1]	226[1]	61
1660 – 69	53	326	341	-15
1670 – 79	82	433	341	92
1680 – 89	69	421	527	-106
1690 – 99	69	365	336	29
1700 – 09	84	388	452	-64
1710 – 19	76	375	388	-13
1720 – 29	70	389	334	55
1730 – 39	61	329	323	6
1740 – 49	70	292	446	-154
1750 – 59	73	249	320	-71
1760 – 69	104	276	307	-31
1770 – 79	126	359	329	30
1780 – 89	131	434	377	57
1790 – 99	199	574	529[2]	45
1800 – 09	321	856	908[3]	-52
1810 – 19	188	717	430[4]	287
1820 – 29	139	756	540	216
1830 – 39	161	698	584	114

[1] registers incomplete for some of these years.
[2] including 132 soldiers or members of their families
[3] including 499 soldiers or members of their families
[4] including 21 soldiers or members of their families

Census, 1801 – 1991

	Males	Females	Total
1801	985	1166	2151
1811	1137	1395	2532
1821	1328	1445	2773
1831	1311	1498	2809
1841	1447	1635	3082
1851	2525	2482	5007
1861	3423	3527	6950
1871	4112	4346	8458
1881	4679	5014	9693
1891	5181	5547	10728
1901	6251	6557	12808
1911	6605	7063	13668
1921	6834	7517	14351
1931	7403	7845	15248

After the extension of the district in 1934 the population was:

	Males	Females	Total
1931	10789	11310	22099
1951	11961	12822	24783
1961	13450	14546	27996
1971	17097	18518	35615

After the extension of the district in 1974 the population was:

	Males	Females	Total
1971	37933	41150	79083
1981	41720	44248	85968
1991	44137	47264	91401

The number of woman exceeded that for men at every census except that for 1851. The larger proportion of men in that year is due to the influx of workers to the railway works, opened in 1847.

Appendix VIII

Workhouse Rules

1770

1. Minute book to be kept of weekly Committee, confirmed at monthly Vestry.
2. No entrants to House unless approved by two of the Committee.
3. All entrants to be cleaned and if necessary clothed.
4. Master to keep peace in the house.
5. All able bodied to work from 6 am to 6 pm in summer, 7 am to 6 pm (or until dark) in winter. Half an hour for breakfast and one hour for dinner.
6. Master to prepare food for breakfast at 8 am, dinner at noon, supper after work.
7. Grace to be said before and after meat. Rooms cleaned daily.
8. Master to keep children clean, with clean linen every Saturday evening.
9. All to be in bed by 9 pm in summer, 8 pm in winter. No smoking except in Common Room
10. Prayers to be said every morning before work, and after supper. Roll called, and absentees punished by the Committee.
11. Master to appoint nurses from the poor, and servants. Reward by Committee, up to 3d per week.
12. Master to give account to Committee every Saturday.
13. Master to keep admission book, with names.
14. Notice to be given to apothecary of sickness.
15. Children to attend school in House from ages 3-6 years. Master appointed by Committee from the poor, and paid up to 6d per week.
16. Girls to be instructed in cooking, washing etc. to qualify them for service.
17. Rooms to be fumigated with wormwood.
18. Account book of household goods etc to be viewed by Committee yearly.
19. No spirits to be allowed in the House.
20. Tradesmen to give details of weights and prices of goods supplied.
21. Poor to attend church (or other religious service) Sunday morning and evening.
22. Vestry clerk to attend Committee meetings and keep books.
23. Children 5-12 years allowed one hour from work to receive instruction in reading.
24. Boxes in House and Church to receive contributions. these to be distributed at Christmas and Easter by Committee to those deserving.
25. All tradesmen's bills to be examined by Committee monthly, and paid by Overseers.
26. Supply of hemp in House for beating by laborious poor in bad weather or when unemployed.
27. Book available in Committee Room for suggestions from parishioners for improvement.
28. Bills of fare now in House to be observed unless altered by Annual Vestry in Easter week.

1786

1. Committee of 30 inhabitants, including churchwardens, overseers, minister and every 'occupier of a hundred a year', to be appointed at Easter to inspect the workhouse and manufacture, etc.
2. At least five of the committee to meet weekly on Thursdays at 10 am.
3. Two of the committee to be appointed monthly to inspect books etc, and to attend committee meetings - to forfeit 1sh, to be excused if a substitute arranged. because of illness etc.
4. Two committee members above to inspect every apartment etc weekly, and to see inmates at dinner.
5. Also to see that a bill is sent for all deliveries.

 6 Retailers of spirituous liquors without licence to be put down, and they or their family not
    to receive relief.
 7 Shops to close on the Sabbath, and no business in any shop after 10 am on that day.
 8 No publican to draw beer, or to allow tippling during divine service, or after 10 pm.
 9 No card playing or other kind of gambling among 'lower sort of people'.
10 No vagrants or trampers in the streets, but to be sent to the cage to beat hemp.
11 No continual relief to single persons (unless under 7 years) above 1s per week, only in case
    of sickness, or two persons living together 1/6d, three people 2/0d, or family 2/6d. No relief
    to bastard children above 7 years, but these to be taken into the House.
12 No weekly relief on account of number of children, but if above three to take those of 7 years
    upward into the House, 'from the certainty their being better brought up'.
13 Overseers to frequently go round the town to enquire after all women suspected to be with
    child of bastard children, to report for action to save Parish expense.
14 No bonfires or fireworks in Town on 5th November. 12 faggots to be given to encourage
    boys to have bonfire in a field.
15 Support magistrates to prevent Players to perform play in Town more than once in 10 years.
16 No encroachment by new buildings over highway.
17 Support to be given to all proposed improvements, these to be approved by at least two thirds
    of the general committee.

Appendix IX

Poor Law Report, 1834

by Ashurst Majendie, Assistant Poor Law Commissioner

Ashford is a considerable town in East Kent, one of the principal markets for the sale of stock and agricultural produce. By means of a select vestry the rates have been reduced to 50%. Weekly wages are 13/6d. In 1820 the rates were 10/0d in the £, and the expenditure £3156. The select vestry has been formed and the full number of 20 members kept up, beside the officers. By their regular attendance the various abuses were detected and the persons and circumstances of the paupers known. The town depends partly on trade and partly on agriculture: the select vestry is chosen from the most respectable in each class who are naturally an assistance and a check on each other. The agriculturists prevent jobbing in the supply of shop goods, and the tradesmen prevent the making up of low wages out of the parish purse. The annual overseers are usually selected from members of the select vestry, and thus have the advantage of a general knowledge of the business of the parish.

Total weekly relief 1822 £1192   1832 £437

There were formerly paid pensions to widows, without due examination of themselves or their children. There is now no fixed pay to widows (unless from infirmity or large families their circumstances require it) and no regular allowance on account of children. Occasional relief is granted when thought requisite, but as a favour and not in the nature of a concession to a demand. Formerly constant pay was given to out-parishioners to prevent them from coming home, and from the fear of not knowing what to do with them. The parish stopped all fixed pay, and made them apply and explain their circumstances, and relieved them according to necessity. No relief is given to resident paupers but on application in person. Respecting those living at a distance, inquiries are made, relief granted for a limited period and fresh applications required. It is thought more desirable to give a sum at once to them than by weekly payments; thus to a journeyman wheelwright living at Canterbury and having 10 children, £6/10/0d was granted to assist him in his rent as an encouragement. At the commencement of the new system an assistant overseer was appointed, but has been discontinued : it is thought it will be requisite to reappoint one. As to men engaged in business, the discharge of the full duty of an overseer is very onerous, and it may not always be possible to find a person competent to keep the accounts in their present state of accuracy.

There is a small workhouse, the inmates are 35 aged or children. Families are sometimes taken in, and the offer of the house made when expe-

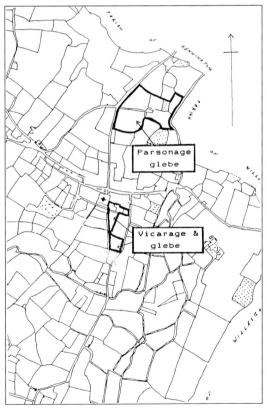

74. *Map showing the Parsonage or Rectory Glebe, and the glebe of the Vicarage.*

dient. Those who are capable are sent out to work at agriculture and handicraft, and the earnings paid to the parish : the expense is 2/8d independent of clothing.

The select vestry meets every week in the committee room in the workhouse, each applicant is heard singly, he withdraws while his case is considered, and the decision is then communicated to him. A few able bodied men are occasionally out of employ, and are set to work under the surveyor of roads. To those living out of the house, relief is given partly in money, partly in flour, potatoes, bread or soup made in the workhouse and delivered out by ticket. Having the advantage of a good market where meat and other necessaries may be procured wholesale, and by economy in cooking, the parish can relieve in provisions at less cost to itself, and with greater advantage to the poor than their own means could supply.

The management of this parish is so good, that applications to the magistrates are very infrequent, and they rarely interfere. The members of the select vestry consider the appeal desirable, as taking part of the responsibility from them.

The practice of paying labourers Fridays instead of Saturdays has been introduced here, and is considered very beneficial. Medical salary £80 includes attendance within the parish. No cottage rents are paid.

Bastardy—maintenance order father 2/0d, mother 9d, invariably enforced of possible.

A Savings Bank has been established, and a Friendly Society—a branch of that in Threadneedle Street. Also a county establishment for the lath of Scray. Labourers contribute to each, and are considered very beneficial.

The good condition of Ashford is the more worthy of note, from its being in the centre of a district in which parishes are extremely oppressed by high and increasing rates.

Appendix X
Grammar School Masters

1635 Baptist Piggott, MA.(Cantab)   1587/1657
   The first master. He was the son of Baptist Piggott of Dartford.

1657 Simon Howe, MA.   ?/1673
   He was also rector of Sevington until 1668, and of Bircholt from 1664 until his death.

1673 Strangford Viall, MA.(Cantab)   1650?/1685
   He was the son of Henry Viall of Ashford, bailiff to the manor. He married in 1685, as his second wife, Jane daughter of Richard Fogge of Dane Court in Tilmanstone, a descendant of the Fogges of Repton. He resigned the mastership in 1679, and became rector of Upminster, Essex until his death.

1679 John Drake, MA.(Cantab)   _c._1652/1712
   He lived in the house called the 'Gatehouse', probably that now 75 High Street, and where had a number of boarders. When he died the inventory of his assets includes a list of the names of those whose boys were at the school, and who had not paid the fees.

1712 Richard Bate, MA.(Cantab)   1685/1749
   · He was son of Rev Stephen Bate, rector of Horsmonden. He was also vicar of Boughton Aluph from 1731 until his death.

1749 Stephen Barrett, MA (Oxon)   1718/1801
   The school attained a high reputation during his period. He resigned the mastership in 1764, but returned two years later. He resigned finally in 1773, when he became rector of Hothfield. He was responsible, with others, for the vesting of a house in the High Street (later 73) in trustees, to be used as a residence for the master and for boarders. He married Mary, daughter of Edward Jacob. An account of Barrett is given in the ' Dictionary of National Biography'.

1764/6 William Hodson, MA.
   Little is known of this master, although he is probably the man who matriculated at Oxford in 1744, aged 19. He appears to have acted in a temporary capacity, perhaps whilst Barrett was absent for some reason.

1773 Charles Stoddart, MA.(Cantab)   1740/1812
   He was also rector of Newchurch from 1785 until his death.

1812 John Nance, MA & DD (Oxon).   1777/1853
   He was the son of William Nance, vicar of Great Chart. He resigned in 1832, when he became rector of Old Romney.

1832 Ephraim Hemmings Snoad, MA.(Cantab) 1794/1856

1856 Robert Henry Wright, MA.(Cantab)   1809/1867

1867 Francis Avarne Dewé, MA.(Cantab)   1838/1888+
   The school was in decline, and did not re-open after the summer recess in 1870

1881 Edward Coulson Musson, MA.(Cantab)   1832/1909
   He was the first master of the new school in Hythe Road. He resigned in 1884.

1884 Benjamin Snell, MA.(Cantab)   1853/1927

1905 John Evans, MA.(Cantab)

1909 Arthur Sydney Lamprey,MA.(Cantab)

1927 Harry Lionel Jenkins 1934 Leslie William White, MA.(Cantab)

1941 Evan Turner Mortimore, MA.(Cantab)

1971 Philip G. Cox, MA.(Cantab)

For further details see R. W. Thomas, _Sir Norton's School_ (1980).

Appendix XI
Church, Charity and Parish Lands

Parsonage land or rectorial glebe

This land, historically described as 24 acres but found in the last century to be about 28 acres, was owned with the manor since very early times. It may be the land granted by Norman de Ashford to Horton Priory in the twelfth century, and then described as 'one virgate of land which Norman gave them and rent of land amounting to ninepence.'

As part of the possessions of Juliana of Leybourne, it passed to the King with the manor in 1362. In 1368 King Edward III granted the advowson to the Leeds Priory (near Maidstone), and this passed to the Crown after that priory was dissolved in 1539. Henry VIII then gave this land for the benefit of the Dean and Chapter of Rochester Cathedral.

The land was leased for farming, usually for periods of 21 years (but renewed every seven years) until 1857, when 8½ acres were sold to the Burial Board to become the 'new' cemetery. In 1875

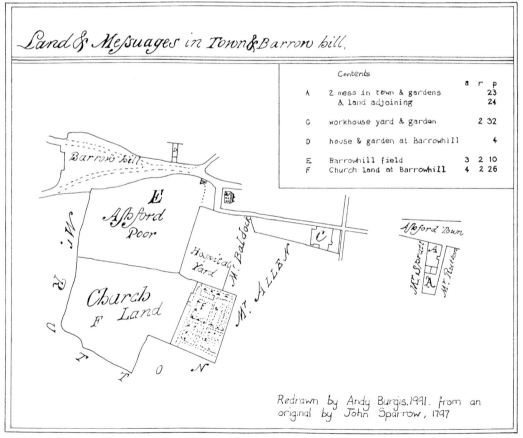

75.   *This and the following maps were drawn by John Sparrow in 1797 of lands held for the benefit of the Church, or for charity purposes. This shows land and houses in the Town and at Barrow Hill.*

the balance of the land was sold to James Salkeld Burra, and subsequently developed for housing.

Vicarage land and glebe

These lands, totalling about 11 acres, have also been owned by the church for very many centuries. As can be seen from the map they originally stretched from the vicarage (called the College) almost to what is today Elwick Road.

About half an acre adjoining Marsh lane (now Station Road) was sold to the parish in 1799 to become the 'new' burial ground. About 6 acres was sold to George Elwick Jemmett about 1820, and in the 1920's all the land south of Vicarage Lane was sold.

Fogge's charity

This land was given by the will of Sir John Fogge, in 1490, and comprised:

The buildings now 83, 85, and 87 High Street, the land now fronting Bank Street on which no. 2 (now National Westminster Bank) and the land adjoining (now a service entrance to County Square)

Land called Cottington originally about seven acres. About one acre was sold to Jemmett in 1820, to pay for the redemption of the land tax, part taken for the railway in 1842, and the balance sold to the Railway Company in 1900.

The right to the first cut of grass in the meadows called Goosepits, Chalmead, Eastmead, Hempsteadmead and Smallmead.

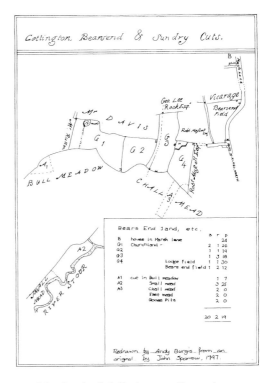

76. *Land called Cottington at Bearsend etc.*

Herbert's charity

There is no record as to when this charity was established. The parliamentary report of 1837 states that in 1574 the lands previously given to the charity, presumably by a man called Herbert, were exchanged for other lands owned by Richard Best.

The land acquired was a farm on the boundary of the parish, and partly in Kingsnorth parish, totalling about 31 acres. It was at one period used as an isolation hospital, and consequently called 'pesthouse farm'. In the last century it was known as Frith farm, and was at times divided into three separate lettings, and was sold by the trustees in 1920. The whole area is now covered by council housing.

Also held by this charity was 4½ acres of land at Barrow Hill. This land was also sold in 1920 for housing development, including Western Avenue, James Street and Eastern Avenue.

Richard Best's charity for the poor

Originally about 3½ acres, but about one acre was sold in 1818 to Pierce Andrews for housing (later to become Barrow Hill Place, Terrace and Cottages), the proceeds being used to redeem land tax. In 1841 part was used for the site of the National school, and subsequently the balance was sold for housing.

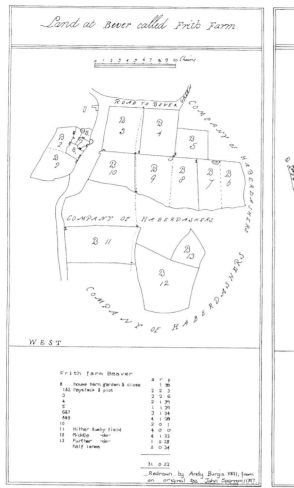

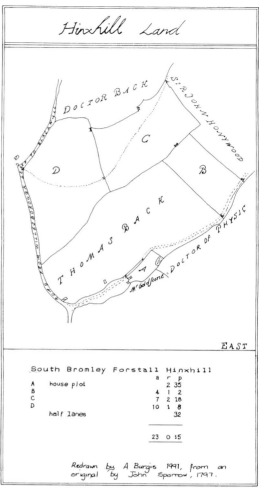

77.   *Land at Beaver called Frith farm.*   78.   *Land at South Bromley Forstall, Hinxhill.*

Asherst charity

This land was given by the will of John Asherst in 1514. It comprised 1½ acres immediately to the south of church lands, fronting Marsh Street (ie. Station Road). On the southern boundary of this land was a cottage used as the tollhouse on the Ashford to Hamstreet turnpike until 1842. The building of the railway necessitated a move, and a new tollhouse was built further south on Beaver Road.

     This land was sold to the Railway Company in 1900.

Martha Copley by her will dated 1663 gave 10 shillings a year, payable by the owner of a house in New Rents, for the benefit of the poor. She lived in Ashford in her widowhood, her husband having been vicar of Pluckley but ejected during the Commonwealth.

William Brett by his will dated 1704, gave £1 a year for the poor, payable from the land called Pellicars.

John Barlow by his will dated dated 1820 gave £100 for the poor.

Grammar school

Norton Knatchbull gave £30 a year for the provision of a grammar school, chargeable on land in Newchurch.

Turner's charity

Dr Thomas Turner, president of Corpus Christi College Oxford, gave 63 acres of land, called Black Forstall in Challock, to provide for the education of both boys and girls of poor people of Ashford. It is not known why this should have been done, as no connection between Turner and the town has been traced. He did , however, have Kentish links as his father, also Thomas, was dean of Canterbury from 1643-72. The land was sold to Lord Gerard in 1894 for £1,500.

Thomas Milles and Sir Richard Smith

£200 was given by the will of Milles in 1625, and £30 by the will of Smith, for the benefit of the poor. With the money, and £20 from parish funds, a cottage and 20 acres of land in Hinxhill were purchased. The property was eventually sold in 1921.

Parish lands

From time to time the Parish owned properties, which were used to provide a workhouse, to house the poor, and as a Bridewell or house of correction (ie a prison).

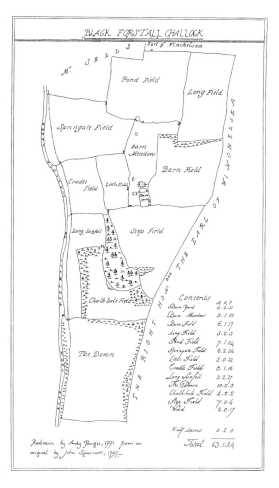

79. Land at Black Forstall, Challock.

The workhouse was in Forge lane, and was built about 1705. The field behind (called Workhouse field) was also owned by the parish. On this land were the National school (until 1841), the parish lock-up, and for some time in the 19th century the fire engine house.

After the workhouse was closed in 1838, the land on which the workhouse stood was sold to John Rolfe, and the land behind to Thomas Nickalls.

From 1711 the parish owned a house at Barrow hill, on part of the land now occupied by the Catholic church, which was used to provide accommodation for poor families. It was sold to Richard Greenhill in 1838.

The Bridewell consisted of four or five cottages in Marsh lane, on the site on which the Baptist church now stands. It was acquired by the parish in 1686. and was sold to the Baptist church in 1838.

Appendix XII
Turnpike Roads

Faversham to Ashford and Hythe, and from Ashford to Canterbury

The roads controlled by this trust are now:

A251   Faversham to Ashford   A261   Newingreen to Hythe
A292 & A20 Ashford to Newingreen   A 28   Kennington (Penlee Point) to Canterbury

The Acts are:

1762   2 Geo III, c.76
1782   22 Geo III, c.102
1803   43 Geo III, c.cix
1824   5 Geo IV, c.lxii
1830   1 Wm IV, c.vi (expired 1863)
1871   34 & 35 Vict c.115 (General Turnpike Act—repealed from 1 November 1871)

There were no turnpikes on this road within the parish of Ashford. No major changes to the existing route within the parish were made by this turnpike.

Financial details
Total loans raised: £9400 Outstanding 1850: £4800

	1834 (£)	1841 (£)	1849 (£)
Cost of repairs	554	865	794
Other expenditure	1141	855	701
Income	1889	1806	1405
Surplus (+) or deficit (-)	194 (+)	86 (+)	90 (-)

Ashford to Bethersden and Tenterden, with branches to Hothfield etc.

The roads controlled by this trust are now:

A28   Ashford to Bethersden and Tenterden
?   Bull Green to Hothfield Heath Bull Green to Dashmanden in Biddenden

The Acts are:

1767   7 Geo III c.103
1786   26 Geo III c.145
1809   49 Geo III c.liv
1819   59 Geo III c.xcvii (expired 1841)
?1880   43 & 44 Vict c.12 (General Turnpike act—repealed from 1 November 1880)

The turnpike on this road within the parish was at Chart Leacon. The site was sold to Lord Hothfield in 1880, for £90.

The original route of this road went from Chart Leacon to Singleton, and then turned sharply north to rejoin Great Chart street at its eastern end. The straight stretch was built around 1800, mainly by military personnel, in order to improve the movement of troops had Napoleon landed in this country.

Financial details
Total loans raised: £5,265   Outstanding 1850: £4264

	1834 (£)	1841 (£)	1849 (£)
Cost of repairs	435	404	382
Other expenditure	433	307	427
Income	954	761	664
Surplus (+) or deficit (-)	86 (+)	50 (+)	145 (-)

Ashford to Stockbridge (south of Hamstreet)

This road is now the A2070

The Acts are:
1793   33 Geo III c.162
1814   54 Geo III c.xxvii (expired 1836)
1879   42 & 43 Vict c.46 (General Turnpike act—repealed from 1 November 1879)

The original turnpike on this road within the parish was at Bear's End, i.e. in what is now Station Road, approximately opposite Dover Place. When the railway was built this gate was abandoned, and a new one constructed in Beaver Road, near the present junction with Bond Road. This was demolished in 1879.

No major changes to the existing route within the parish were made by this turnpike.

Financial details
Total loans raised: £3,100   Outstanding 1850: £2,800

	1834 (£)	1841 (£)	1849 (£)
Cost of repairs	201	207	253
Other expenditure	265	172	147
Income	470	333	409
Surplus (+) or deficit (-)	4 (+)	46 (-)	9 (+)

Ashford to Maidstone

This road is now the A20

The Acts are:
1793   33 Geo III c.173
1814   54 Geo III c.xviii
1836   6   Wm IV c. 1 (expired 1868)]
1869   32 & 33 Vict c.90 (General Turnpike act—repealed from 1 November 1879)

The turnpike road on this road in the parish was at Potter's Corner, and is the only one of those on any turnpike in the parish which still exists. It was sold to Lord Hothfield in 1859 for £50, and is still used as a private house.

The original route of this road went down what is now Warren lane to Sparrow's Hall before turning back to join the present route towards the crest of the hill before Potter's Corner. This change was made about 1800, and the alteration is clearly shown on the Ordnance map of that date.

The Act of 1836 transferred that portion of the road between Barrowhill and the 'Castle' inn from the Tenterden Trust to this one, It also authorised the purchase and demolition to widen the road of three properties on the east corner leading to the High Street, occupied by Stephen Hodges, Thomas Back and Mary Hart, and vested in the devisees of William Allen, postmaster, deceased.

Financial details
Total loans raised: £8,258   Outstanding 1850: £4,290

	1834 (£)	1841 (£)	1849 (£)
Cost of repairs	906	729	591
Other expenditure	626	1165	294
Income	1575	1894	1039
Surplus (+) or deficit (-)	43 (+)	–	154 (+)

Appendix XIII
Coach Routes 1838 and 1874

In 1838 the following routes were running:

1   W Gilbert & Co., 'Times' coach, London to Folkestone, daily from the *Saracen's Head*
    London   8 am   arr Ashford   3.15 pm   arr Folkestone   5.30 pm
    Folkestone   8.30 am   arr Ashford   10.30 am   arr London   5 pm

2   Packham van, Ashford to Maidstone, daily from the *George*
    Ashford   6 am   arr Maidstone   11.30 am
    Maidstone   7 pm   arr Ashford   midnight

3   Packham van, Dover to Maidstone from the *George*
    Dover   9 am   arr Ashford   2 pm   arr Maidstone   5.30 pm

4   Benton van, Maidstone to Dover, daily from the *George*
    Maidstone   10 am   arr Ashford   1.30 pm   arr Dover   5.30 pm
    Dover   8.30 am   arr Ashford   11.30 am   arr Maidstone   2.30 pm

5   Benton van Folkestone to Ashford, Monday, Wednesday and Friday
    Dover   10 am   arr Ashford   2 pm

6   Kennett van (Chatham, via) Maidstone to Dover, daily
    Maidstone   9.30 am   arr Ashford   2 pm   arr Dover   7 pm
    Dover   8 am   arr Ashford   1 pm   arr Maidstone   5.30 pm

7   Lusted van, Ashford to Canterbury, daily from the *George*
    Ashford   9 am   arr Canterbury   11 am
    Canterbury   4 pm   arr Ashford   6 pm

8   Randall van, Canterbury to Ashford, daily
    Canterbury   10.30 am   arr Ashford   12.30 pm
    Ashford   2 pm   arr Canterbury   4 pm

9   Bill's van, Faversham to Ashford, Tuesday, Thursday & Saturday from the *George*
    Faversham   10 am   arr Ashford   1 pm
    Ashford   2 pm   arr Faversham   5 pm

10 Cadwell 'Reliance' coach, St Leonards to Dover, via Ashford
    from St Leonards   Tuesday, Thursday & Saturday
    from Dover   Monday, Wednesday & Friday
    St Leonards 8.30 am   arr Ashford   12.45 pm   arr Dover   3 pm
    Dover   10.30 am   arr Ashford   1 pm   arr St Leonards 5 pm

11 Blacklock, Lydd to Ashford, daily from the *George*
    Lydd   8.30 am   arr Ashford   noon
    Ashford   2 pm   arr Lydd   5.30 pm

12 Wraight, Brookland to Ashford, Tuesday
    Brookland   ?
    Ashford   2 pm   arr Brookland   4.45 pm

13 Fagg, Warehorne to Ashford, Friday
    Warehorne   ?
    Ashford   2 pm   arr Warehorne   4.15 pm

In 1874 the railway was available from London, and to Canterbury, Folkestone and Hastings. This meant that the coaches on these routes were no longer necessary, but the importance of Ashford as a centre for the surrounding district can be seen in the transport available to the smaller towns and villages.

The directory for that year lists: omnibuses and flys from the *Saracen's Head* meet every train; omnibuses to Maidstone and Tenterden daily, and to Faversham and Woodchurch daily except Sundays; carriers to Aldington, Appledore, Bethersden, Biddenden, Bilsington, Bonnington, Boughton Aluph, Brabourne, Canterbury, Challock, Charing, Chilham, Cranbrook, Dymchurch, Egerton, Faversham, Folkestone, Great Chart, Hamstreet, Hothfield, Hythe, Ivychurch, Kennington, Lenham, Little Chart, Lydd, Maidstone, Mersham, New Romney, Pluckley, Ruckinge, Rye, Sandgate, Shadoxhurst, Smarden, Smeeth, Stowting, Tenterden, Westwell, Woodchurch and Wye.

Services were provided as follows:

Name	From	To	S	M	T	W	T	F	S
Austin	*Marlborough*	Dymchurch, New Romney & Lydd			★			★	
Barling	*George*	Bilsington & Ruckinge			★			★	
Blackman	*George*	Faversham			★		★		★
Blackman	*George*	Wye		★		★		★	
Buss	*New Inn*	Hothfield & Pluckley			★		★		★
Checksfield	20 New Street	Hythe & Folkestone		★		★		★	
Cheesman	*George*	Charing		★		★		★	
Collins	*New Inn*	Boughton Aluph			★				
Coppins	*New Inn*	Egerton			★				
Coulter	*George*	Kennington & Wye		★	★	★	★	★	★
Day	*George*	Egerton			★		★		★
Hook	*Market*	Cranbrook			★		★		★
Hook	*Market*	Tenterden	★	★	★	★	★	★	★
Horne	*George*	Bilsington & Bonnington			★			★	
Jennings	*New Inn*	Hothfield & Charing	★	★	★	★	★	★	
Kingsland	*Marlborough*	Smeeth & Brabourne			★				
Law	*George*	Appledore & Rye			★				
Leaver	*New Inn*	Ham Street, Ivychurch, Dymchurch New Romney & Lydd			★			★	★
Lee	*George*	Chilham & Canterbury			★			★	★
Link	*New Inn*	Great Chart & Bethersden			★			★	★
Lonkhurst	*George*	Ham Street	★	★	★	★	★	★	★
Lonkhurst	*George*	Rye						★	
Newton	*Royal Oak*	Charing, Lenham & Maidstone	★	★	★	★	★	★	★
Pearson	*New Inn*	Charing & Smarden		★		★		★	
Pellatt	*British Volun.*	Biddenden & Maidstone		★					★
Rogers	*Saracen's Head*	Challock & Faversham	★	★	★	★	★	★	★
Simpson	*Marlborough*	Dymchurch & New Romney			★		★		
Spice	*George*	Kennington				★			
Stone	*Marlborough*	Aldington & Bilsington			★		★		
Summers	*Somerset Arms*	Boughton Aluph & Challock			★		★		
Turner	*George*	Shadoxhurst & Woodchurch	★	★	★	★	★	★	★
Wanstall	*George*	Mersham & Aldington			★		★		★
Wood	*Swan*	Smeeth, Brabourne & Stowting			★				
Wood	*Swan*	Westwell & Charing			★			★	★
Wood	*George*	Little Chart & Smarden			★		★		★
Woodcock	*George*	Great Chart & Bethersden			★		★		★
		Total journeys	6	12	29	12	17	19	18

The number of departures from each inn was: *British Volunteer*, 1; *George* inn, 16; *Market* hotel, 2; *Marlborough* inn, 4; *New Inn*, 7; *New Street*, 21; *Royal Oak*, 1; *Saracen's Head*, 1; *Somerset Arms*, 1; *Swan*, 2. Total: 36.

Appendix XIV

Inns

Details are given in chapter eleven of the major inns in the town towards the end of the 18th century. There were in addition many smaller houses which only lasted whilst one individual carried on his trade. When he died those premises were closed and someone else would open, perhaps only a few doors away. The details below are of those that existed in the 17th and 18th centuries. Very few of those listed exist today, either as businesses or even as buildings.

Red Lyon was the inn in North Street that was renamed the *Lord Roberts* early in this century, and was demolished to make way for the extension of Park Street. It certainly existed from the 17th century.

Crown was an important inn in its time, on the site that is now 12/18 High Street. It ceased to be an inn about 1760, when a new mansion for one of the Mascall family was built on the site.

Ounce's Head. An odd name, but the explanation is that the ounce or snow leopard was the crest on the arms of the Strangfords, whose family were lords of the manor from about 1558 to 1708. It must therefore have been named in their honour during that period. This inn was in the lower High Street in the building now no.31.

Royal Oak was in the lower High Street on the site now occupied by Pearl Assurance Co. The building that was there until the 1970s (last used by Olby's the ironmongers) was built about 1730. One record suggests that an earlier inn of the same name, but much smaller, existed a few doors away. If it started earlier than 1660 it must have had another name, since the Royal Oak was only acceptable after the restoration of Charles II. It was one of the more important inns in its time, used by farmers attending the cattle market held in the High Street. The corn market was held there from the middle of the 18th century until the opening of the Corn Exchange in 1860.

Chequers was also in the lower High Street, and part of the building still survives in the courtyard behind 25 High Street, and known as 'Whitehall'. The building that is there now marks the probable original street frontage—the market place being much wider than today. These premises ceased to be an inn about 1700.

Pied Bull. This must have been a very large inn in the 17th century. It occupied the building in the High Street now used by Worgers, but the building was originally much larger, including the site now 73 High Street.

White Hart—in the upper High Street, on the site later 93-95. It was renamed the *Fountain* about 1845, and demolished about 1870.

Castle at the top of the High Street. The present building is relatively recent, but there has been an inn on this site since at least the 17th century. The origin of the name is obscure, and for a time in the 18th century the name was changed to *King's Head.*

Marlborough at the top of East Hill—demolished when the ring road was constructed. As an inn or alehouse, this dates from at least the early 18th century, as the name indicates. On land to the rear there was a brewery, perhaps from a much earlier date, which continued until the middle of the last century.

Other premises that are known include:

Swan. It is almost certain that the site now 80 (and perhaps also that of 78) High Street was an inn of this name until the early 18th century. A passage way from the High Street to the land at the rear previously existed between these two buildings, as with the *George* and the *Saracen's Head.*

Bull or *Naked Boy* or *Star*, now 69/71 High Street.This inn had a cockpit in the 18th century, and organised matches of cockfighting against teams from neighbouring towns.

King's Head, next door at 67. This was at one time the posthouse, where the mail would be received.

Turk's Head, now 63 High Street. At the end of the 15th century this house belonged to the widow of Sir John Fogge.

Six Bells, on the corner of the churchyard entrance, becoming 55 High Street.

Bell, a very small building in St John's Lane, behind 19 High Street.

Drum, on the corner of New Rents and Hempstead Street, demolished for the Tufton Centre shopping complex.

Plough. The burial register records the burial on 20 October 1701 of 'a stranger at the Plow'. This must have been an inn, but no other reference has been found.

And lastly, there were several places out of the town centre, including:

Fountain, the building now the *Prince of Orange* in New Street, but not used as an inn for about one hundred years from the middle of the 18th century.

Rose & Crown at Barrow Hill, on part of the site of the Catholic Church today.

Trumpet, on the south side of the river, on the road to Beaver.

Hare and Hounds at Potter's Corner, called *Fox and Hounds* until the beginning of the 19th century. These premises belonged to the lord of the manor until about 1760.

Even allowing for the fact that all of these premises were not open at the same time, there was plenty of choice for Ashfordians in the past to get a drink, despite all the restrictions the Justices tried to impose.

Unfortunately, we know very little of the individual landlords who ran the inns, apart from their names. The importance of the *Saracen's Head* is shown by the landlords who, over a long period, appeared in the Courts (held opposite in the room over the market buildings) whenever an extra witness was required. No doubt those coming to the town would stay there, and preliminary discussions between the lawyers and the witnesses would take place. Perhaps the landlord joined in!

In some cases the premises were run by the same family for several generations. For example, the *George* was held by a family called Clare from about 1600 to 1720.

In the early 16th century there seems to have been something of a family 'closed shop' in innkeeping in Ashford. A James Mascall was the landlord of the *Saracen's*. He had two daughters, both of whom married 'in the trade'. His wife Ann was probably the brother of a Peter Colbrand, who later held the *Saracen's*, followed by his son Thomas. But Peter Colbrand married a Judith Bayliffe, whose first husband Francis was the landlord of the *Pied Bull*, and who was related by marriage to the Clares of the *George*. What would be interesting to find out is whether these complex family relationships led to great rivalry, or whether they conspired together to the detriment of their customers. Alas, we are never likely to be able to find the answer.

Appendix XV

Improvement Commissioners

Improvement Commissioners

Justices of the Peace residing in Ashford and the Vicar were members *ex officio*

	from	to
Thomas Allen	★	20 March 1839
Alexander Apsley	20 March 1839	27 October 1847 disqualfied
John Apsley	31 May 1824 ★	20 March 1839
Richard Barnes	19 December 1849	12 September 1850
John Bayley	20 March 1839	elected to Board 1863
John Beet	★	
James Bond (vicar)	31 May 1824 ★	September 1826 deceased
John Udall Bugler	23 January 1861	elected to Board 1863
William Burra JP	19 December 1849	
Philip Boghurst	★	20 March 1839
George Wm Cartwright	27 October 1847	19 December 1849
William Cobb	?	27 October 1847
Charles Cordeaux	★	
William Cruttenden	19 December 1849	
William Culling	19 December 1849	August 1854 deceased
Abraham Dangerfield	19 December 1849	
Charles Dorman	23 January 1861	elected to Board 1863
John Dorman	23 January 1861	not elected to Board 1863
Mark Dorman	★ appointed Treasurer	
John Dungey		27 October 1847 left parish
George Elliott	★	1863. Did not seek election
George Elliott jun.	12 September 1850	elected to Board 1863
John Elliott	31 May 1824 ★	1861 deceased
Thomas Elliott	19 December 1849	1858 deceased
William Flint	28 June 1824 ★	
William Flint jun.	8 May 1845	
Robert Furley	6 December 1833	appointed clerk 1852
David B. Green	19 December 1849	5 May 1856 resigned
Richard Greenhill sen.	★	March 1829 deceased
Richard Greenhill jun.	31 March 1836	5 May 1856 resigned
Charles Haffenden	31 May 1824 ★	20 March 1839
Thomas Haffenden	★	20 March 1839
Henry Headley	19 December 1849	elected to Board 1863
John Hutton	31 May 1824 ★	
Henry Illesley	★ appointed Clerk	
William R. Jeffery	22 May 1845	
George Elwick Jemmett	31 May 1824 ★	16 March 1829 disqualified
William Jemmett	31 May 1824 ★	February 1828 dec'd
William Jemmett jun.	15 May 1845	19 December 1849
James Lewis	20 March 1839	
Richard Lewis	21 June 1833	27 October 1847 disqualified
William Morley	2 June 1834	23 January 1861 resigned
John Nance	★	16 March 1829 disqualified

Charles Norwood	★	20 March 1839
Francis Norwood	31 May 1824 ★	18 November 1830
George Paine	22 May 1845	27 October 1847 left parish
William Parnell	31 May 1824 ★	
Alexander Power	16 September 1825	
Peter Rabson	31 May 1824 ★	28 June 1824
Henry P. Ramsay	19 December 1849	
Lewis Ambrose Reeve	11 November 1840	5 May 1856 resigned
David Rist	23 January 1861	
James Rogers	20 March 1839	August 1852 deceased
Henry Loftie Rutton	16 September 1825	27 October 1847 left parish
Henry Scott	5 November 1856	
William Scott	16 July 1833	19 December 1849
William Sheppard	19 December 1849	not elected to Board 1863
Edward W. Simonds	19 December 1849	
John Startup	21 October 1830	
Thomas Startup	21 October 1830	27 October 1847 disqualfied
Charles Stoddart	★	
Edward Stoddart	?	19 December 1849
George Stonham	19 December 1849	
John Taylor	23 January 1861	elected to Board 1864
Benjamin Thorpe	10 September 1824	19 December 1849
Benjamin Kelly Thorpe	19 December 1849	elected to Board 1863
Richard Thorpe	5 May 1856	elected to Board 1864
Thomas Thurston	19 December 1849	
Henry Alfred Tite	23 January 1861	elected to Board 1868
John Tunbridge	18 November 1830	19 December 1849
Stephen Tunbridge	31 March 1836	19 December 1849
James Wal	14 June 1824	19 December 1849
William Walter sen.	31 May 1824 ★	
William Walter jun.	8 June 1845	
Henry Whitfeld	22 May 1845	elected to Board 1863
William Whitfeld	14 June 1824	20 March 1839
George Fredk Wilkes	22 May 1845	not elected to Board 1863
John Worger	16 September 1825	
John Worger jun.	11 November 1840	elected to Board 1863

★ named in Act

Officers

Clerk
1824	Henry Illesley	@ £15 p.a. for first two years, then £10 p.a.
1827	John Cullen Knott	@ £10 p.a. and Inspector of Nuisances from 1848
1852	Robert Furley	@ £10 p.a.
1858		reduced to £7 p.a. on appointment of rural police

Treasurer
| 1824 | Mark Dorman | @ £5 p.a. |
| 1860 | Francis Creed Thurston | @ £5 p.a. |

Collector
1852 Francis Pain @ £10 p.a.

Local Board

under Local Government Act, 1858 (adopted 10 March 1863)
The results of the first election:

	votes	
John Allen	286	
John Bayley	489	resigned 1 May 1863 when not elected Chairman
Edmund Burnett	338	
John Udall Bugler	488	
Charles Dorman	452	
William Dungey	305	
George Elliott jun.	469	resigned 1 May 1863 because of ill-health
George Foord	370	
George W. Greenhill	492	
Charles S. Hammond	346	
Henry Headley	364	
George Lepine	413	
John Mead Linom	356	
Richard C. Mansell	478	
Richard Rabson	428	
Thomas Ebenezer Scott	368	
John Fitch Spicer	479	
Thomas John Startup	417	
Benjamin Kelly Thorpe	477	
Henry Whitfeld	421	
John Worger	417	

The following 13 men stood for election, but were not successful James Benton, William Pomfret Burra, John S. Coombes, John Dorman, James S. Eastes, Henry Foster, John C. Goldberg, David B. Green, John Russell Lewis, Walter Murton, John Dobree Norwood, William Sheppard, and George Frederick Wilks. Walter Murton and John Dobree Norwood were elected in place of John Bayley and George Elliott.

The following were members during the period 1863-1894

		from	**to**
John Allen	cabinet maker	1863	1872
Henry E. Austen	wine merchant	1888	end
Joseph Batchelor		1892	end
John Bayley	auctioneer	1863	1863
John Henry Bayley	auctioneer	1871	1877
William Beet	doctor	1877	1885
George Beken	saddler	1884	1890
James Benton	farmer	1880	end
John Broad	tallow chandler	1880	end
William R. Brown	publican	1887	end
John Udall Bugler	ironmonger	1863	1865
		and 1872	1887
Edmund Burnett	saddler	1863	1867
Frank T. Cantrell	mill manager	1889	1892
Ebenezer Chapman	brewer	1878	1893
Charles Clemetson	draper	1877	1880
George Cobb	publican	1881	1884
John Cooper	tailor	1880	1883

James I'Anson Cudworth	railway engineer	1864	1877
Charles Dorman	currier	1863	1875
William Dungey	ironmonger	1863	1863
Thomas Edwards	publican	1876	end
William H. Edgar		1887	end
George Elliott jun.	brewer	1863	1863
Thomas Lewis Elliott	brewer	1873	1887
Jonathan Fife	baker	1887	1890
George Finn	furnisher	1868	1877
George Foord	engineer	1863	1871
James Fraser	solicitor	1874	1888
Joseph Gage	grocer	1885	1889
George W. Greenhill	tanner	1863	1882
Charles S. Hammond	draper	1863	1868
Charles W. Hammond	draper	1882	1884
William G. Handcock		1887	end
George Harper	furnisher	1882	end
Charles Harrison	baker	1884	1893
Alfred Hart	corn merchant	1879	1880
William Fowler Harvey	grocer	1880	end
George H. Hayward	butcher	1868	1871
Henry Headley	grocer	1863	1874
Isaac Hendy		1879	1882
Frederick Hyland	draper	1864	end
Richard James	publican	1891	end
Henry James Jeffery	architect	1892	end
Henry Knock	builder	1885	end
George Knowles	furnisher	1888	end
George Lepine	grazier	1863	1872
John Russell Lewis	maltster	1866	1878
John Mead Linom	grocer	1863	1878
Richard C. Mansell	railway engineer	1863	1868
Edward Marshall	publican	1893	end
William Marshall	coachbuilder	1871	1872
		and 1875	1891
John Maxted	farmer	1891	end
Walter Murton	farmer	1863	1864
John Dobree Norwood	solicitor	1863	1889
Arthur Parrock	draper	1872	1875
William Pledge	miller	1890	end
Peter Rabson	draper	1885	1889
Richard Rabson	draper	1863	1872
William Rabson	draper	1872	1881
Walter M. Richardson	brewer	1889	1892
Thomas Ebenezer Scott	tailor	1863	1871
George A. Spain	grocer	1877	end
John Fitch Spicer	farmer	1863	1879
Thomas John Startup	farmer	1863	1864
John Taylor	draper	1864	1869
		and 1875	1887
Richard Thorpe		1864	1865
Edward Whitfeld Thurston	doctor	1877	1874
Henry Alfred Tite	draper	1868	1877

William Wainwright	railway engineer	1883	1893
James Waterman		1884	1893
James Watson		1877	1885
Henry Whitfeld	doctor	1863	1869
George Fredk Wilks	doctor	1864	1879
George Wilks	doctor	1892	end
Frederick Worger		1871	1885
John Worger	grocer	1863	1874
Charles Askey Wotton		1889	end

Chairmen
1863   George Lepine (John Bayley resigned from the Board after being defeated in the voting for
       Chairmanship)
1872   James I'Anson Cudworth
1874   Charles Dorman
1875   John Udall Bugler
1887   Thomas Edwards
1892   William G. Handcock

Urban District Council

Elections for the first council were held on 17 December 1894. The town was divided into three
wards—North, Central and South, each electing six members. The number of voters in each ward
was 487, 643 and 670 respectively. At the first meeting, held on 2 January 1895, William Handcock
was elected as the first chairman.

North ward

elected			not elected		
George Alfred Spain	grocer	387	Henry James Jeffery	architect	133
George Wilks	doctor	311	William Pledge	miller	131
George Knowles	furnisher	254	William Marshall	coachbuilder	58
Robert Sidney Gibbs	draper	246	William Henry Watkins	leather seller	35
George Harper	furnisher	190	Thomas Deverson		21
Walter M. Richardson	brewer	159			

Central ward

William G. Handcock		462	Frederick B. Solly		195
Richard James	publican	392	Edward Sigrist	insur super	157
Thomas Edwards		364	William W. Sayer		133
John Broad	chandler	361			
William R. Browne	publican	349			
Henry Edward Austen	wine merch.	321			

South ward

William G. Deness	grocer	421	Henry Knock	builder	280
John Andrew Rutter	reporter	380	W. Mapperson		271
Edward Marshall	publican	362	Thomas Rossiter	publican	256
William F. Harvey	grocer	331	W. Heckles		108
John Barling	shopkeeper	317	William George Vile		96
Joseph Batchelor		282			

Italics indicate members of old Board.

James Benton, William Edgar, Frederick Hyland, John Maxted and Charles Wooton were
members of the old Board but did not stand for election.

Local Board and first Urban District Council Officers

Clerk
1863	Robert Furley	£30 p.a. + £5 for contested elections
1871	Frederick Hughes Hallett	£10 p.a. + £20 for contested elections
from 1876		£60 p.a.
1897	John Creery	£250 p.a.

Treasurer
1863	Elisha Davis	£7 p.a.
from 1877		£10 p.a.
from 1892		£25 p.a.
1897	Thomas Nottidge	no salary

Collector
1863	Francis Paine	£20 p.a.
1864	Thomas Young	£20 p.a.
1868	Harry H. Stickings	£20 p.a.
1871	Jonah Lorden	£20 p.a. (also Inspector of Nuisances)
1876	Charles E. Homewood	£20 p.a.

Surveyor
1863	Thomas Thurston	£50 p.a.
1877	Charles Doswell	£150 p.a.
1878	Arthur Sidney Robinson	£150 p.a.
1885	John Willson	£150 deceased 1891
1892	William Terrill	£150 p.a.
from 1894		£200 p.a.

Medical Officer of Health
1873	William Sheppard	£25 p.a.
1878	William H. Coke	£15 p.a.
1892	Richard Bevan	£40 p.a.

from 1893 additional £20 p.a. for superintendence of sanatorium

Inspector of Nuisances
1870	Jonah Lorden	£70 p.a. (also Collector)
1877	combined with duties of Surveyor	

Inspector of Lodging Houses
1866	Thomas Dunk (police sergeant)	£1 p.a.
1868	Joy (police sergeant)	£2 p.a.

Appendix XVI
Postmasters

	1675	Robert (although referred in Treasury Books as Edward) Lott, dismissed for neglect 1677	
	1677	James Rufford	
by	1685	Alexander Hart	*Naked Boy* [71] High Street
Mar	1695	Thomas Lake	
	1697	Samuel Farrow	
Feb	1697/8	William Clare	*George*, High Street
Jan	1709/10	John Reeve	? [7-9] High Street
Jul	1716	John Smith	
	1729	John Smith jun.	
	1730	Edmund Barnar	
	1734	John French	*Royal Oak*, High Street
	1750	Mary French	
	1760	Thomas French	?*King's Head* [67] High Street
	1769	Robert Wood[1]	[60] High Street
	1780	Stephen Kemsley [2]	*George*, High Street
	1795	John Bayley	
	1798	John Reader	
	1805	William Allen[3]	? High Street
Sep	1818	John Tunbridge	[41 & 43] High Street
	1861	John Edw Munns	47-49 High Street
	1870	John Edw Munns	Bank Street (now National Westminster Bank)
Dec	1893	Thomas Chas Hooke	
Jun	1904	Frederick Wm Norman Smith	
Jul	1911	George Cooper	
Mar	1918	F.J. Taylor	
Apl	1921	Tufton Street post office opened	
Nov	1926	C.W. Clarke	
Aug	1931	W. Shade	
Apl	1946	Percy C.L.H. Bulmer	

[1] In 1773 Daniel Bodkin was charged at Quarter Sessions with having stolen money 'from the post office of Robert Wood, grocer'.

[2] Although Stephen Kemsley was appointed and is given in official records as the postmaster, he moved to Maidstone very soon after the appointment. The Post Office objected to the operation by a substitute, who was presumably Simon Peverel and then Thomas Ratcliff, who succeeded Kemsley at the *George*.

[3] The Turnpike Act of 1836 (6 Wm IV c.l) authorised purchase and demolition of property on east corner of Castle lane leading to High Street, owned by devises of William Allen, postmaster, in order to widen the road.

Appendix XVII

Major Fires in Ashford before 1939

25 Dec 1836	Farm buildings, Jeffery Benton, Barrowhill.
1843	Stables, rear of 26 & 28 New Street.
1850	Builders' yard, Draper Fowler, rear of 96 High Street.
26 Jan 1858	Carpenters' shop etc, rear of Queen's Head, East Hill.
27 Aug 1864	Stables, rear of 26 & 28 North Street.
18 Sep 1865	Corn store, shop & houses, 12, 14 & 16 and *Old Prince of Wales*, New Street.
29 Sep 1867	3 houses, 18, 20 & 22 New Street.
16 Oct 1869	Lion brewery, Dover Place.
9 Apl 1870	Factory, Edmund Burnett, rear of 30 High Street.
21 Jun 1874	Carriage works, Wm Marshall 38 New Street. ?
14 Aug 1876	*New Inn*, 26-28 New Street.
11 Mar 1877	House at Millbridge [Hythe Road]—5 persons killed.
9 Jun 1877	Shop, John Howland, 12 Bank Street.
13 Oct 1877	5 new houses, Hardinge Road.
1 Mar 1879	Sawmills, Draper Fowler, rear of 32 Bank Street.
4 May 1879	Wheelwrights' shop, Joseph Hartfield, 87 New Street.
2 Dec 1879	Houses, 86, 88 & 90 New Street.
12 Jan 1880	Grocer's shop, Henry Headley, 46 High Street.
4 Nov 1880	Oil merchant's shop, Samuel Williamson, 13 High Street.
1 Dec 1882	Draper's shop, William E. Buss, 1 & 3 High Street.
8 Nov 1883	Shop, John Reeve, 24 High Street.
22 May 1884	Shop, Thomas Scott, 77 High Street.
10 May 1885	Shop, Freeman, 22 & 24 New Street
10 Jul 1885	House, 3 Whitfeld Road.
9 Feb 1887	House, 9 Hempstead terrace [Godinton Road]—2 children killed.
14 Mar 1887	Workshop, Wm Ball, rear of 20 New Street.
1 Dec 1887	Store, occupied by George Andrews, rear of 76 New Street.
12 Nov 1888	Ironmonger's shop, George Hearden, 28 Bank Street
13 Apl 1891	*Kentish Express* printing works, Park Street.
11 Jun 1891	Currier's shop, St John's Lane (rear of 19 High Street).
15 Jul 1891	Kelway & Marsh, 82 High Street.
11 Jan 1894	Pipe works, John Phillips, 91 New Street.
18 Jan 1896	House, 3 Church Road.
21 Dec 1897	Shop, Lewis & Hyland, 11 New Rents.
6 Aug 1901	Shop, Charles Read, 21 New Rents.
10 Sep 1901	Marine store, William Maldram, 67 New Street.
29 Oct 1902	Edward's Motor works, 43 Station Road.
4 Sep 1903	Hampton or Hampden Court farm, Beaver.
5 Aug 1904	Shop, Henry Headley, 44 High Street.
7 Apl 1906	Timber yard, Frank Davis, Station yard.
14 Sep 1906	Printing works, Headley Bros., Edinburgh Road.
16 Mar 1908	House, Taylor's passage [High Street]—woman aged 88 years killed.
27 May 1908	Timber yard, Frank Davis, Station yard.
16 Aug 1911	Timber yard, Henry Knock, Queen's Road.
3 Jun 1912	Shop, Maypole Dairy, 83 High Street.
16 Apl 1913	Victoria Flour Mills, Victoria Road.

8 Nov 1914   Hayward's motor works, 32 New Street.
15 Apl 1915   Victoria Flour Mills, Victoria Road.
29 Jun 1918   3-storied house, 12 Gravel Walk.
14 Mar 1926   Co-operative Society store, 24–28 High Street.

In addition to attending fires in the town the brigade was available when required to deal with outbreaks in the surrounding villages, and some of the largest fires occurred in the rural areas. In September 1872 it assisted with a serious fire in Canterbury Cathedral.

The increase in their work can be judged by the following summary of the total number of call-outs to incidents:

1828–29	1	1890–99	61
1830–39	5	1900–09	104
1840–49	9	1910–19	80
1850–59	13	1920–29	158[1]
1860–69	23	1930–39	194[2]
1870–79	33	1940–42	79
1880–89	49		

[1]   No figures available for 1925.
[2]   No figures available for 1937, 1938 or 1939.

Bibliography

Primary sources

The following groups of documents are the main source of the details in this book, all of which are in the Centre for Kentish Studies, Maidstone, unless noted otherwise.

Parish registers of births, marriages and deaths. (held by the vicar, but available on microfilm)

Wills —Archdeaconry Court	PRC 17
—Consistory Court	PRC 32
—Prerogative Court (Public Record Office)	PRO 11
Inventories—Archdeaconry Court	PRC 10
Quarter Sessions —Papers	Q/SB
—Order Books	Q/SO
Bridge papers	Q/AB & Q/GA
Victuallers licences	Q/RLv
Ashford Manorial records	U 1045/M1 - 20 etc.
Minute books —Improvement Commissioners 1824-1863	U 1045 O7
—Local Board and Urban District Council	UD/AS Am1
Map of Ashford by James Gouge, 1818	DRc/EP1
Tithe apportionment and map, 1843	P10/27

Secondary sources

Books on the history of Ashford.
Box, E. S., *Ashford Congregational Church* (1962)
Briscall, Walter, 'The Ashford Cage' in *Arch. Cant.*, Vol .101 (1984)
Briscall, Walter, *Discovering Ashford's Old Buildings* (1987)
Filmer Richard, *Old Ashford*, (1983)
Filmer, Richard, *Ashford in old Photographs* (1988)
Furley, Robert, *Home Reflections* (1867)
Furley, Robert, 'Early History of Ashford' in *Arch. Cant.*, Vol. 16 (1884)
Hasted, Edward, *History of Kent*, Vol. 7 (1798)
Hussey, Arthur, *Ashford Wills, 1461-1558* (1938)
Igglesden, Chas, *Ashford Church* (1901 etc.)
Igglesden, Chas, *A Saunter through Kent*, Vol. 34 (1946)
Local History Group, *Ashford's Past at Present* (reprinted 1982)
Local History Group, *Seventeenth Century Ashford* (1980)
Mills, Mark, *Doctor George Wilks* (1970)
Mortimore, E.T., *Sir John Fogge and Ashford Church* (1970)

Palmer, A.E.W., *History of Ashford Fire Brigade* (1987)

Pearman, A.J., *Ashford, its Church,* etc. (1868, 1886 & 1904)

Rochard, J., *Ashford: Illustrated and Historical* (1898)

Roberts, Rev. E., revised by V.G. Clark, *History of the Baptist Church* (1978)

Ruderman, Arthur, and Filmer, Richard, *Ashford: A Pictorial History* (1991)

St John's Ambulance, *Ashford Corps Centenary* (1979)

Thomas, R.W., *Sir Norton's School* (1980)

Toke, John, *Five Letters on the State of the Poor* (1808)

Turner, Gordon, *Ashford: The Coming of the Railway* (1984)

Various, *Ashford: a Record of 500 years* (1970)

Wallenberg, J.K., *Kentish Place-names* (1931)

Wallenberg J.K., *Place-names of Kent* (1934)

Warren, W.M., *History of Ashford Church* (*c.*1712, printed 1895)

Watson, A.C., *History of Religious Dissent in Ashford* (1979)

Weeks, W.A., *Baptist Church of Ashford* (1931)

Wood, J.H., *The Martyrs of Kent* (1885)

Newspapers
Ashford & Alfred News, 1855-1861 when it was re-named *Kentish Express & Ashford News*.

Except for those published in the last few years, many of these books are out of print, but most can be seen in the Ashford Library, Reference Room.

Index

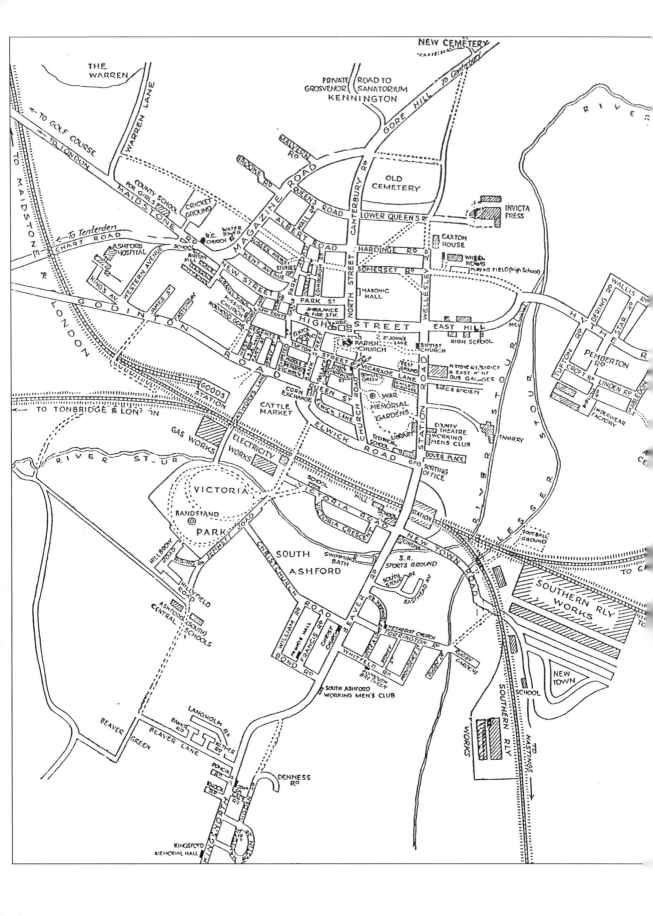